This Rum Tasting Log Book

Belongs to

_____

DEDICATION

This Rum Tasting Log Book is dedicated to all the Rum Lovers out there who are mindful of tasty drinks and want to have fun in the process.

You are my inspiration for producing books and I'm honored to be a part of keeping all of your thoughts and ideas organized all in one easy to find spot.

How to use this Rum Tasting Log Book:

This ultimate rum tasting notebook is a perfect way to track and record all your tasty activities. This unique rum tasting journal is a great way to keep all of your important information all in one easy to find spot.

Each interior page includes prompts and space to record the following:

1. Name - Write the name of which rum you are tasting.

2. Distiller - Use the box provided to write in who made it, or what company.

3. Origin - Stay on task using the box to fill in where in the world this rum was made.

4. Color Meter- Record and track the color of the rum that is being sampled, from clear to black

5. Flavor Wheel - Checklist what flavor was sampled, anywhere from woody to spicy.

6. Additional Notes - Space to write additional thoughts and ideas.

7. Final Rating - Fill in checklist star rating from 1-5 on appearance, taste, mouthfeel and overall rating.

If you are new to tasting rum or have been at it for a while, this rum tasting journal is a must have! Can make a great useful gift for anyone that aspires to be a rum tasting sommelier!

Have Fun!

	NAME		
	DISTILLERY		TYPE
	ORIGIN		AGE
	PRICE		SAMPLED

COLOR METER

- CLEAR
- –
- STRAW
- –
- HONEY
- –
- GOLD
- –
- AMBER
- –
- MAHOGANY
- –
- BLACK

FLAVOR WHEEL

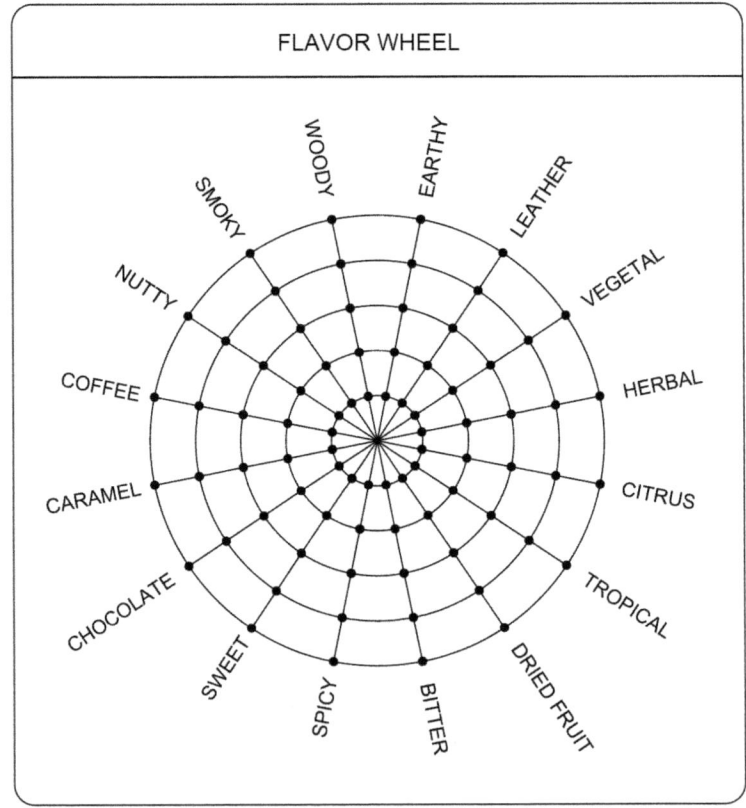

SMOKY, WOODY, EARTHY, LEATHER, NUTTY, VEGETAL, COFFEE, HERBAL, CARAMEL, CITRUS, CHOCOLATE, TROPICAL, SWEET, SPICY, BITTER, DRIED FRUIT

ADDITIONAL NOTES

FINAL RATING

- APPEARANCE ☆☆☆☆☆
- TASTE ☆☆☆☆☆
- MOUTHFEEL ☆☆☆☆☆
- OVERALL RATING ☆☆☆☆☆

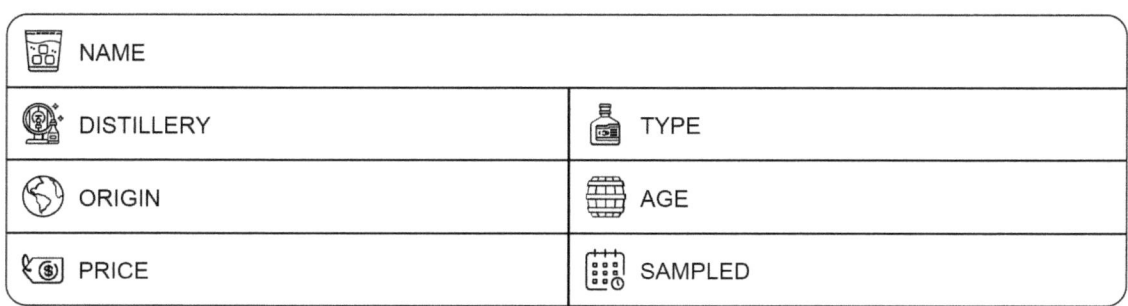

	NAME		
	DISTILLERY		TYPE
	ORIGIN		AGE
	PRICE		SAMPLED

COLOR METER

- CLEAR
- STRAW
- HONEY
- GOLD
- AMBER
- MAHOGANY
- BLACK

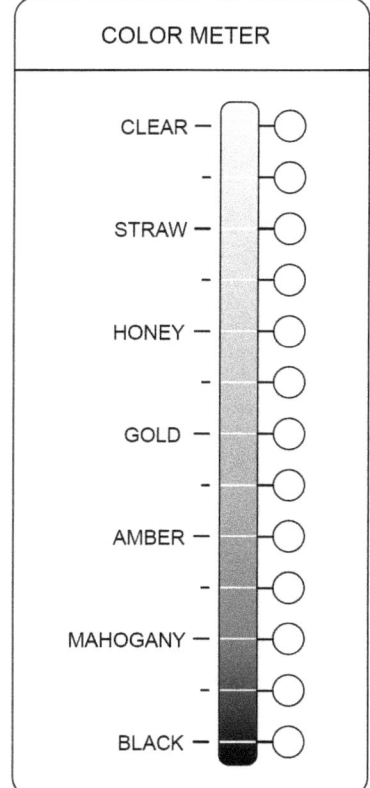

FLAVOR WHEEL

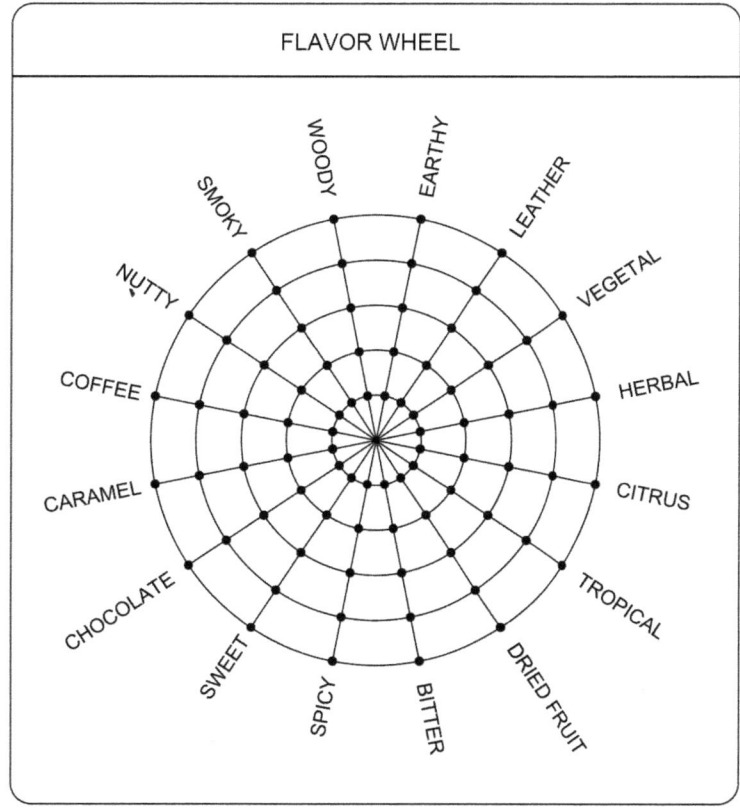

SMOKY · WOODY · EARTHY · LEATHER · VEGETAL · HERBAL · CITRUS · TROPICAL · DRIED FRUIT · BITTER · SPICY · SWEET · CHOCOLATE · CARAMEL · COFFEE · NUTTY

ADDITIONAL NOTES

FINAL RATING

- APPEARANCE ☆☆☆☆☆
- TASTE ☆☆☆☆☆
- MOUTHFEEL ☆☆☆☆☆
- OVERALL RATING ☆☆☆☆☆

NAME			
DISTILLERY		TYPE	
ORIGIN		AGE	
PRICE		SAMPLED	

COLOR METER

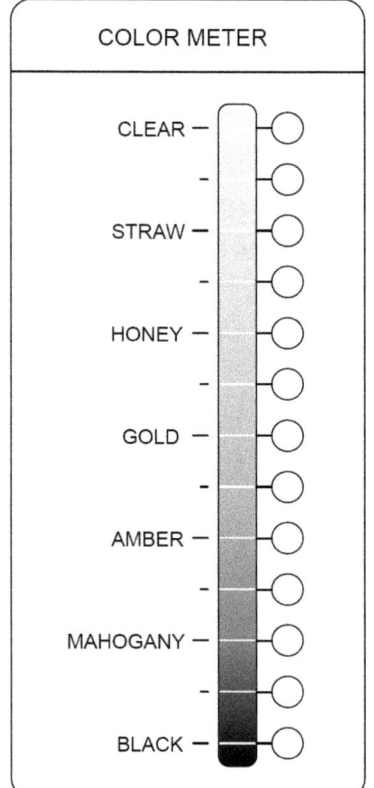

FLAVOR WHEEL

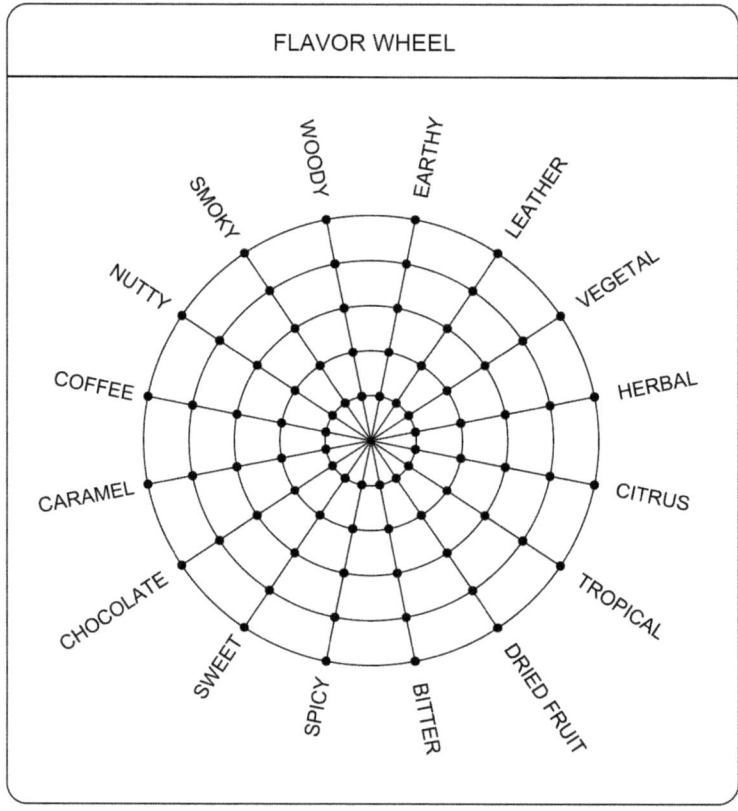

ADDITIONAL NOTES

FINAL RATING

- APPEARANCE ☆☆☆☆☆
- TASTE ☆☆☆☆☆
- MOUTHFEEL ☆☆☆☆☆
- OVERALL RATING ☆☆☆☆☆

NAME	

DISTILLERY		TYPE	
ORIGIN		AGE	
PRICE		SAMPLED	

COLOR METER

- CLEAR
- —
- STRAW
- —
- HONEY
- —
- GOLD
- —
- AMBER
- —
- MAHOGANY
- —
- BLACK

FLAVOR WHEEL

SMOKY, WOODY, EARTHY, LEATHER, NUTTY, VEGETAL, COFFEE, HERBAL, CARAMEL, CITRUS, CHOCOLATE, TROPICAL, SWEET, SPICY, BITTER, DRIED FRUIT

ADDITIONAL NOTES

FINAL RATING

- APPEARANCE ☆☆☆☆☆
- TASTE ☆☆☆☆☆
- MOUTHFEEL ☆☆☆☆☆
- OVERALL RATING ☆☆☆☆☆

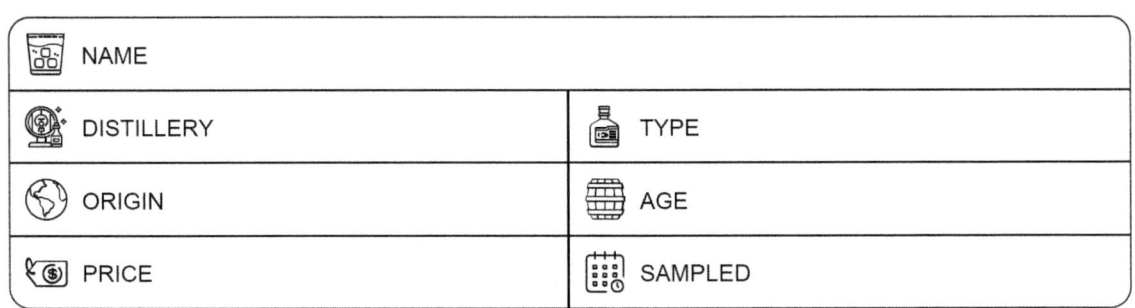

NAME			
DISTILLERY		TYPE	
ORIGIN		AGE	
PRICE		SAMPLED	

COLOR METER

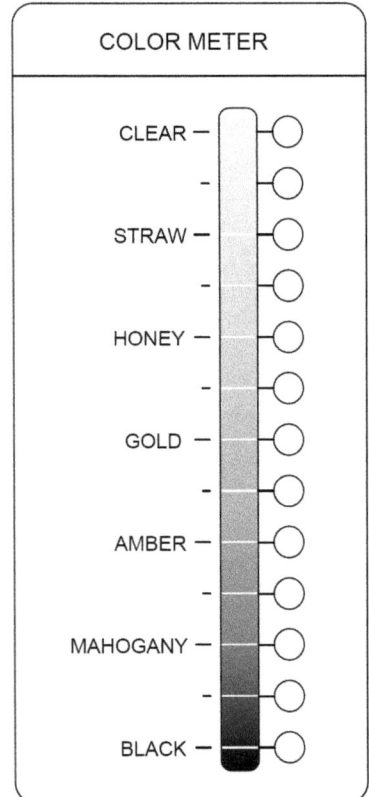

- CLEAR
- STRAW
- HONEY
- GOLD
- AMBER
- MAHOGANY
- BLACK

FLAVOR WHEEL

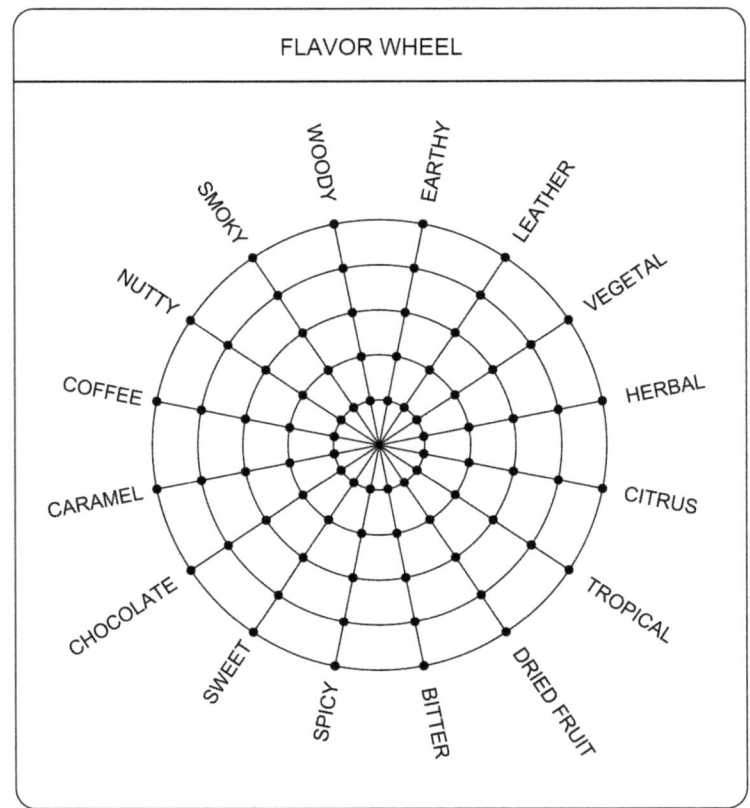

SMOKY, WOODY, EARTHY, LEATHER, NUTTY, VEGETAL, COFFEE, HERBAL, CARAMEL, CITRUS, CHOCOLATE, TROPICAL, SWEET, SPICY, BITTER, DRIED FRUIT

ADDITIONAL NOTES

FINAL RATING

- APPEARANCE ☆☆☆☆☆
- TASTE ☆☆☆☆☆
- MOUTHFEEL ☆☆☆☆☆
- OVERALL RATING ☆☆☆☆☆

	NAME		
	DISTILLERY		TYPE
	ORIGIN		AGE
	PRICE		SAMPLED

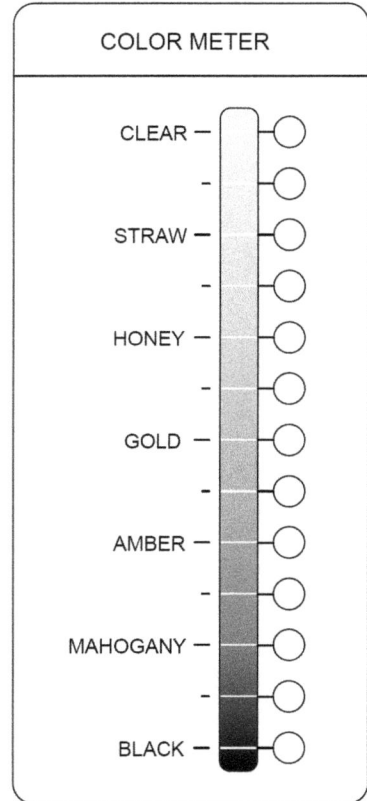

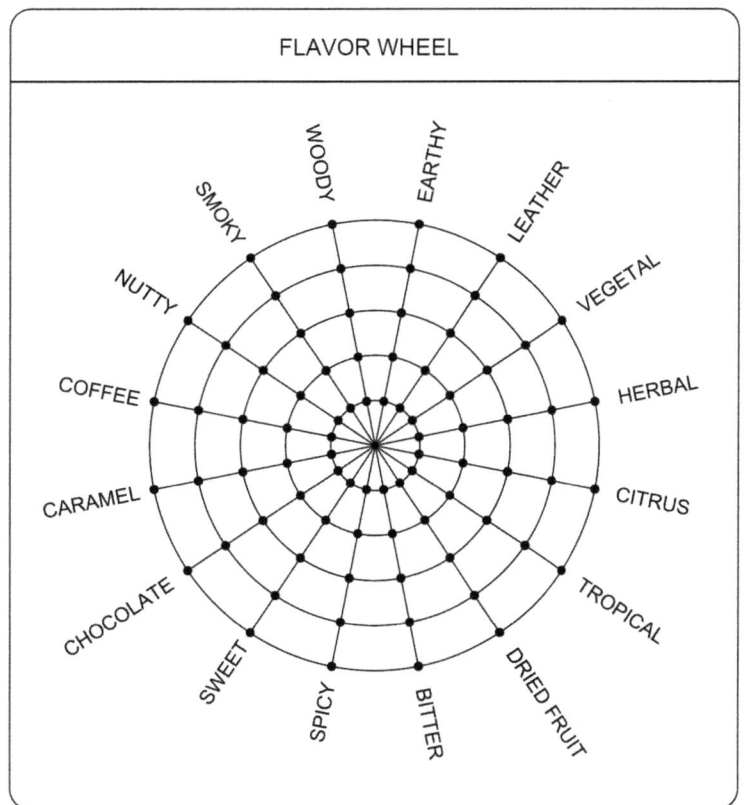

ADDITIONAL NOTES

FINAL RATING

- APPEARANCE ☆☆☆☆☆
- TASTE ☆☆☆☆☆
- MOUTHFEEL ☆☆☆☆☆
- OVERALL RATING ☆☆☆☆☆

	NAME		
	DISTILLERY		TYPE
	ORIGIN		AGE
	PRICE		SAMPLED

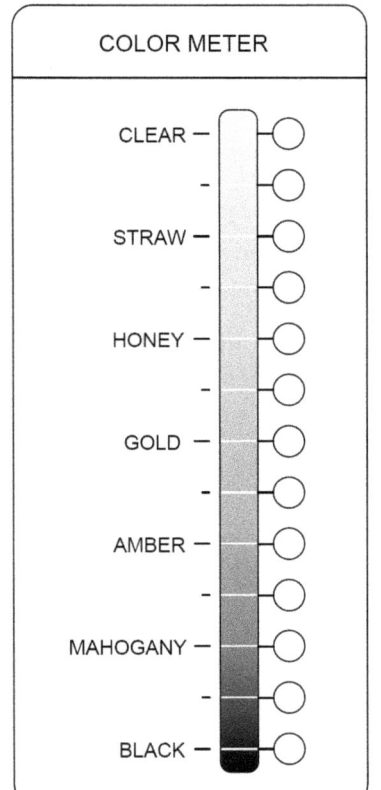

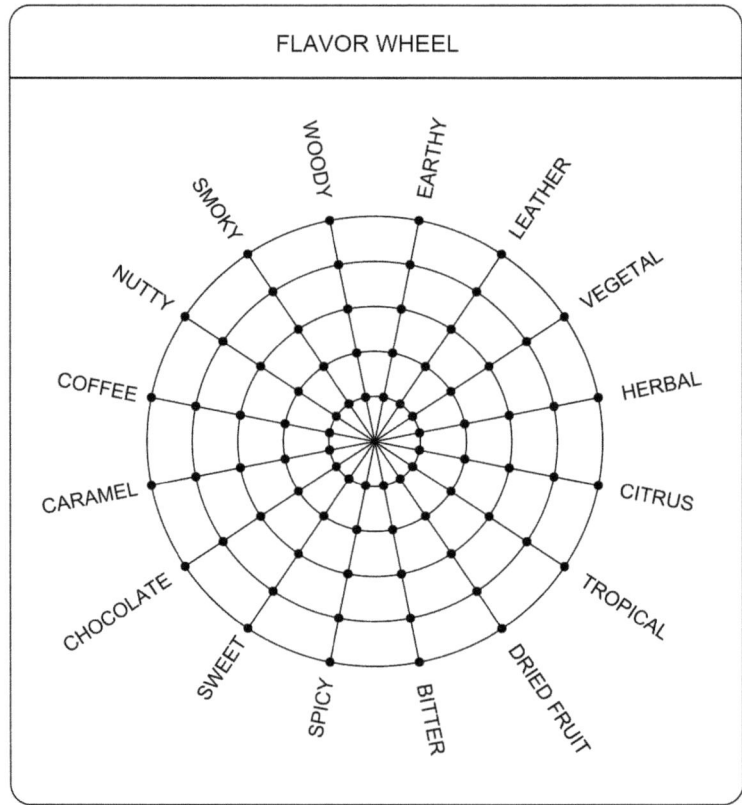

ADDITIONAL NOTES

FINAL RATING

- APPEARANCE ☆☆☆☆☆
- TASTE ☆☆☆☆☆
- MOUTHFEEL ☆☆☆☆☆
- OVERALL RATING ☆☆☆☆☆

NAME	

DISTILLERY		TYPE	
ORIGIN		AGE	
PRICE		SAMPLED	

COLOR METER

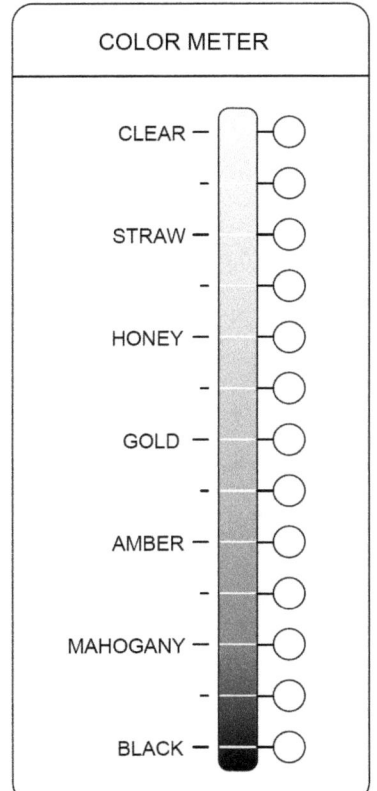

- CLEAR
- STRAW
- HONEY
- GOLD
- AMBER
- MAHOGANY
- BLACK

FLAVOR WHEEL

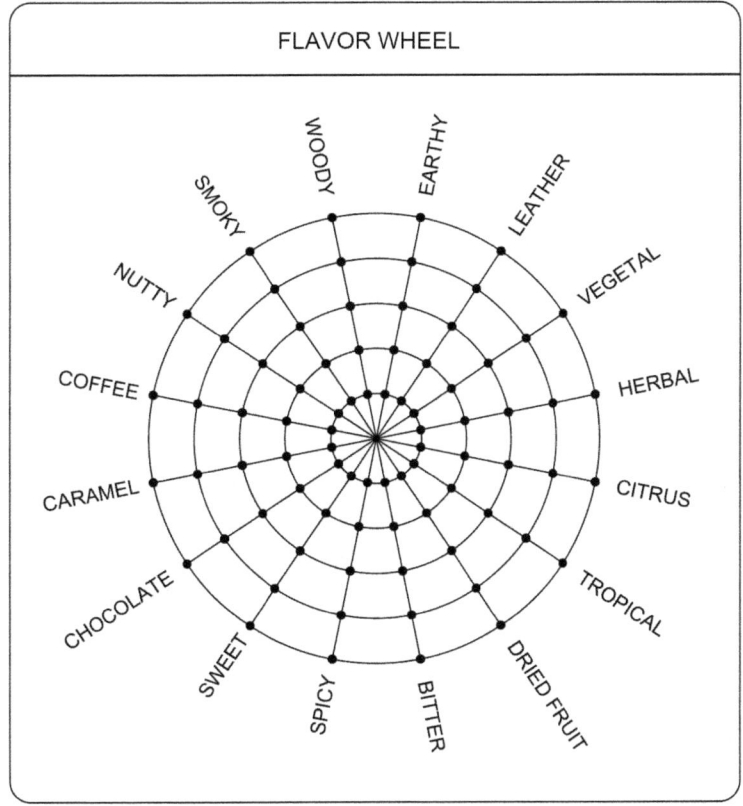

SMOKY, WOODY, EARTHY, LEATHER, NUTTY, VEGETAL, COFFEE, HERBAL, CARAMEL, CITRUS, CHOCOLATE, TROPICAL, SWEET, SPICY, BITTER, DRIED FRUIT

ADDITIONAL NOTES

FINAL RATING

- APPEARANCE ☆☆☆☆☆
- TASTE ☆☆☆☆☆
- MOUTHFEEL ☆☆☆☆☆
- OVERALL RATING ☆☆☆☆☆

	NAME		
	DISTILLERY		TYPE
	ORIGIN		AGE
	PRICE		SAMPLED

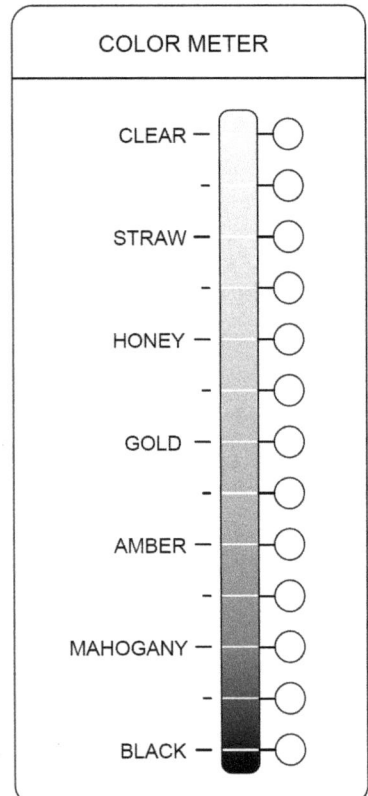

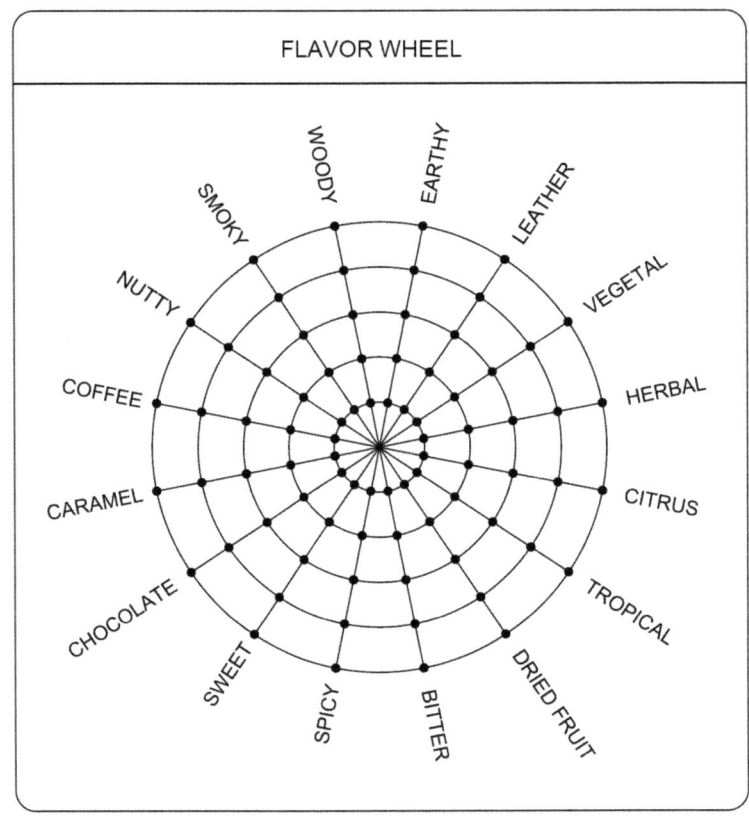

ADDITIONAL NOTES

FINAL RATING

- APPEARANCE ☆☆☆☆☆
- TASTE ☆☆☆☆☆
- MOUTHFEEL ☆☆☆☆☆
- OVERALL RATING ☆☆☆☆☆

	NAME		
	DISTILLERY		TYPE
	ORIGIN		AGE
	PRICE		SAMPLED

COLOR METER

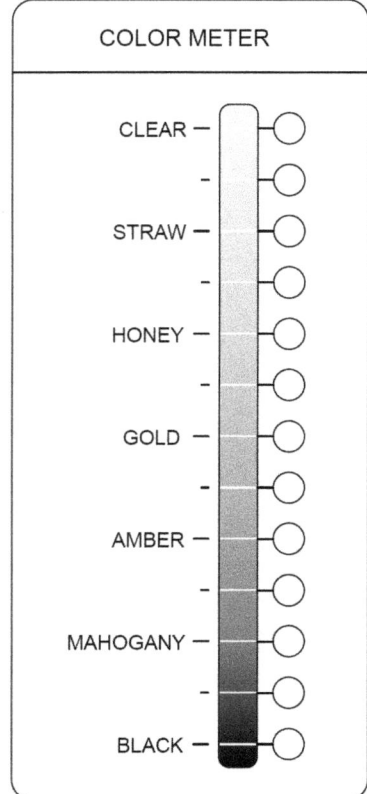

- CLEAR
- STRAW
- HONEY
- GOLD
- AMBER
- MAHOGANY
- BLACK

FLAVOR WHEEL

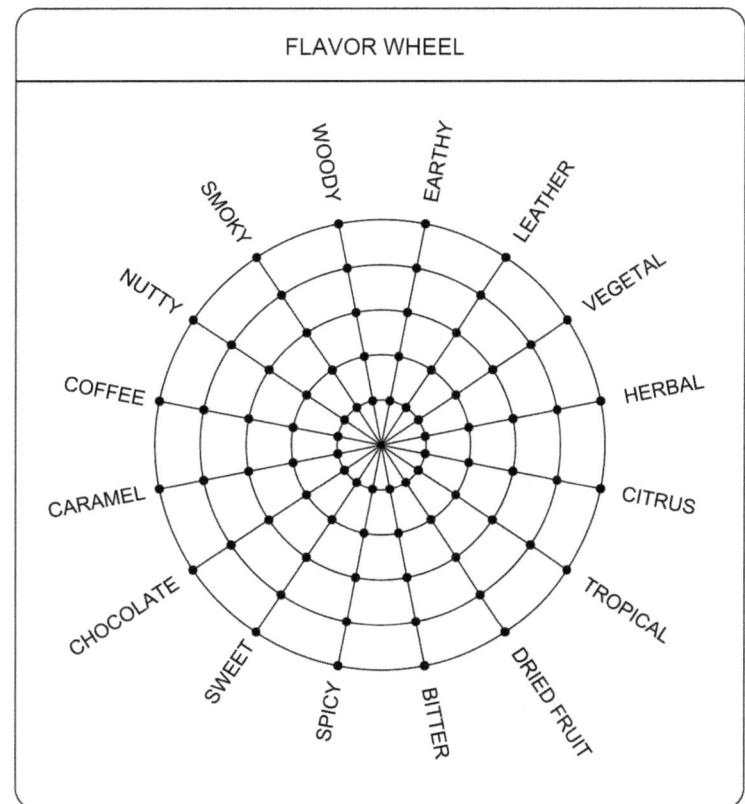

WOODY, EARTHY, LEATHER, VEGETAL, HERBAL, CITRUS, TROPICAL, DRIED FRUIT, BITTER, SPICY, SWEET, CHOCOLATE, CARAMEL, COFFEE, NUTTY, SMOKY

ADDITIONAL NOTES

FINAL RATING

- APPEARANCE ☆☆☆☆☆
- TASTE ☆☆☆☆☆
- MOUTHFEEL ☆☆☆☆☆
- OVERALL RATING ☆☆☆☆☆

	NAME		
	DISTILLERY		TYPE
	ORIGIN		AGE
	PRICE		SAMPLED

COLOR METER

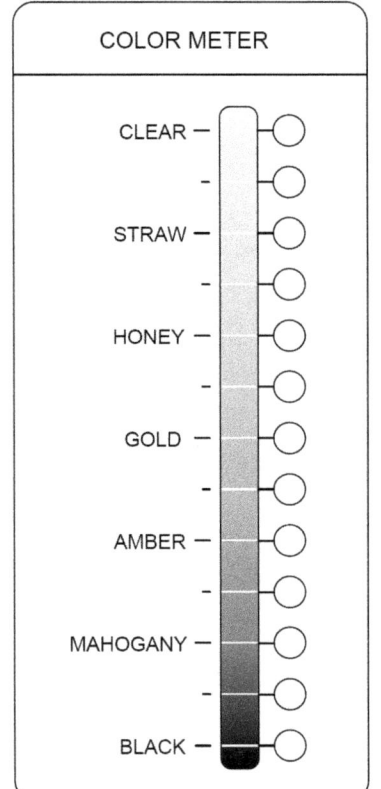

- CLEAR
- STRAW
- HONEY
- GOLD
- AMBER
- MAHOGANY
- BLACK

FLAVOR WHEEL

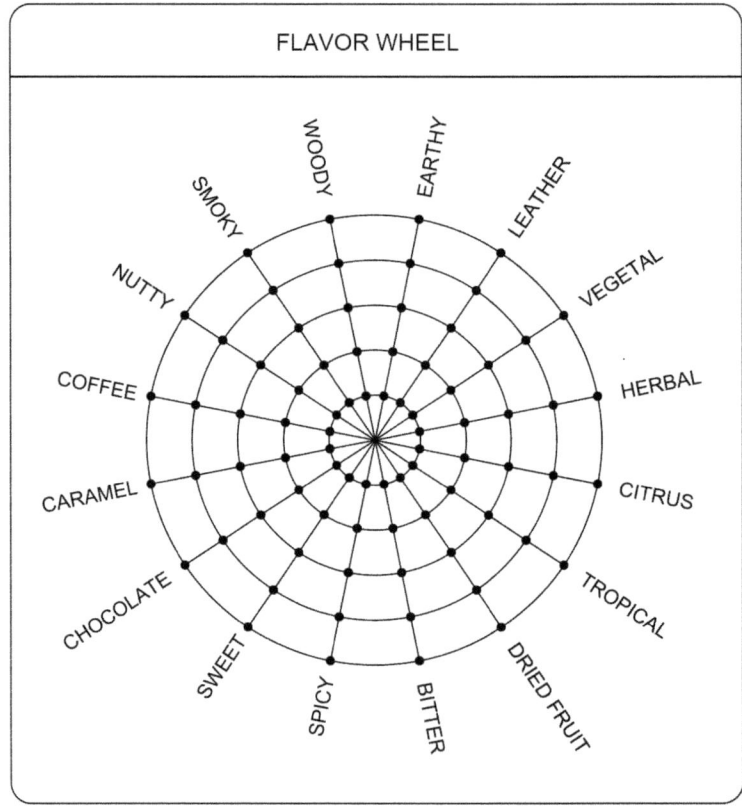

SMOKY, WOODY, EARTHY, LEATHER, VEGETAL, HERBAL, CITRUS, TROPICAL, DRIED FRUIT, BITTER, SPICY, SWEET, CHOCOLATE, CARAMEL, COFFEE, NUTTY

ADDITIONAL NOTES

FINAL RATING

- APPEARANCE ☆☆☆☆☆
- TASTE ☆☆☆☆☆
- MOUTHFEEL ☆☆☆☆☆
- OVERALL RATING ☆☆☆☆☆

NAME	
DISTILLERY	TYPE
ORIGIN	AGE
PRICE	SAMPLED

COLOR METER

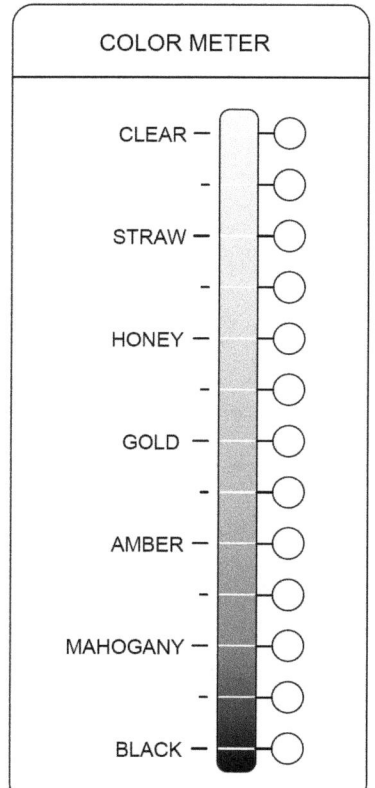

- CLEAR
- STRAW
- HONEY
- GOLD
- AMBER
- MAHOGANY
- BLACK

FLAVOR WHEEL

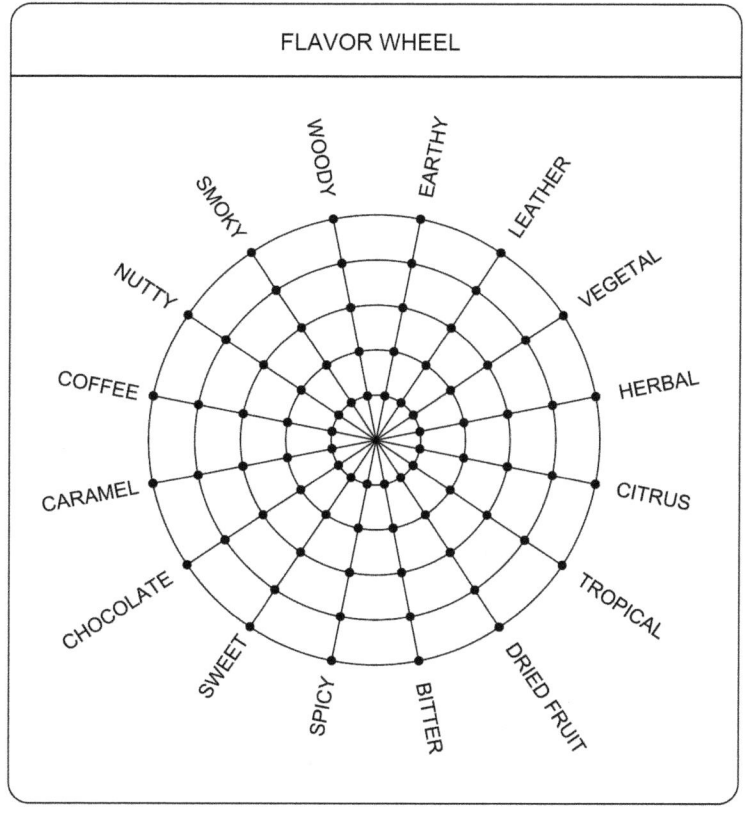

SMOKY, WOODY, EARTHY, LEATHER, NUTTY, VEGETAL, COFFEE, HERBAL, CARAMEL, CITRUS, CHOCOLATE, TROPICAL, SWEET, SPICY, BITTER, DRIED FRUIT

ADDITIONAL NOTES

FINAL RATING

- APPEARANCE ☆☆☆☆☆
- TASTE ☆☆☆☆☆
- MOUTHFEEL ☆☆☆☆☆
- OVERALL RATING ☆☆☆☆☆

NAME			
DISTILLERY		TYPE	
ORIGIN		AGE	
PRICE		SAMPLED	

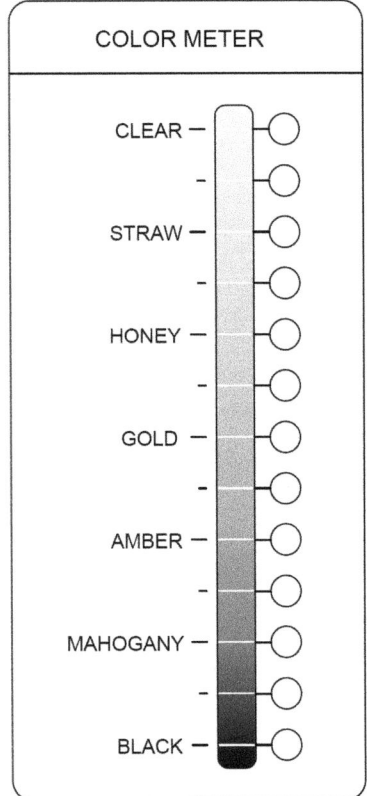

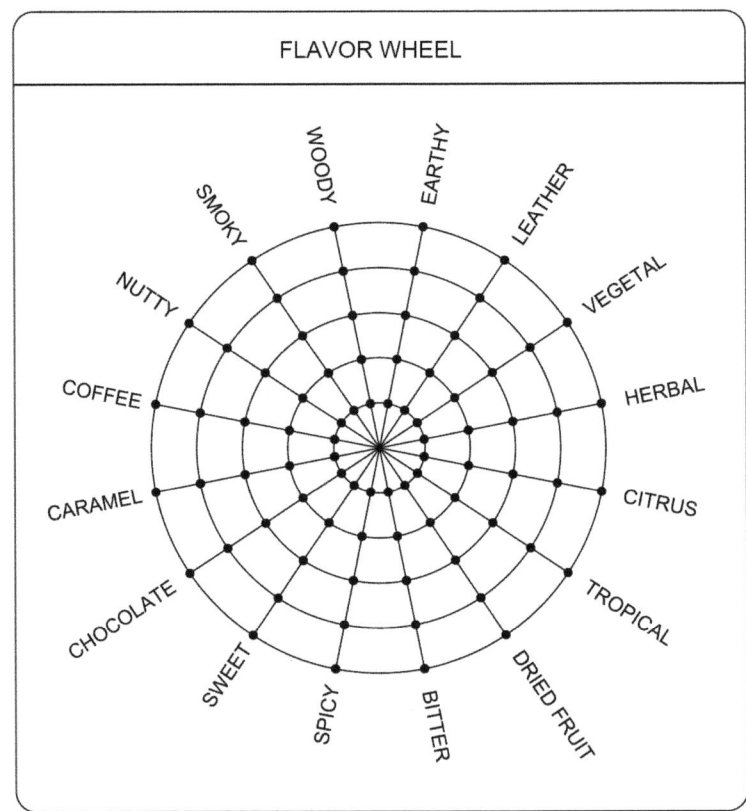

ADDITIONAL NOTES

FINAL RATING

- APPEARANCE ☆☆☆☆☆
- TASTE ☆☆☆☆☆
- MOUTHFEEL ☆☆☆☆☆
- OVERALL RATING ☆☆☆☆☆

	NAME		
	DISTILLERY		TYPE
	ORIGIN		AGE
	PRICE		SAMPLED

COLOR METER

- CLEAR
- STRAW
- HONEY
- GOLD
- AMBER
- MAHOGANY
- BLACK

FLAVOR WHEEL

SMOKY, WOODY, EARTHY, LEATHER, VEGETAL, NUTTY, HERBAL, COFFEE, CITRUS, CARAMEL, TROPICAL, CHOCOLATE, DRIED FRUIT, SWEET, SPICY, BITTER

ADDITIONAL NOTES

FINAL RATING

- APPEARANCE ☆☆☆☆☆
- TASTE ☆☆☆☆☆
- MOUTHFEEL ☆☆☆☆☆
- OVERALL RATING ☆☆☆☆☆

NAME

DISTILLERY	TYPE
ORIGIN	AGE
PRICE	SAMPLED

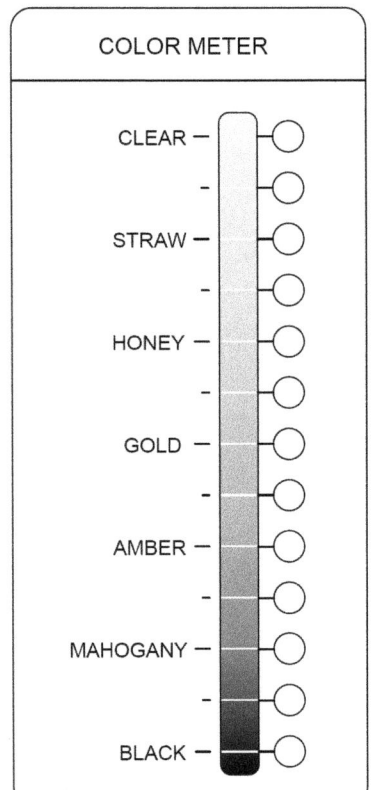

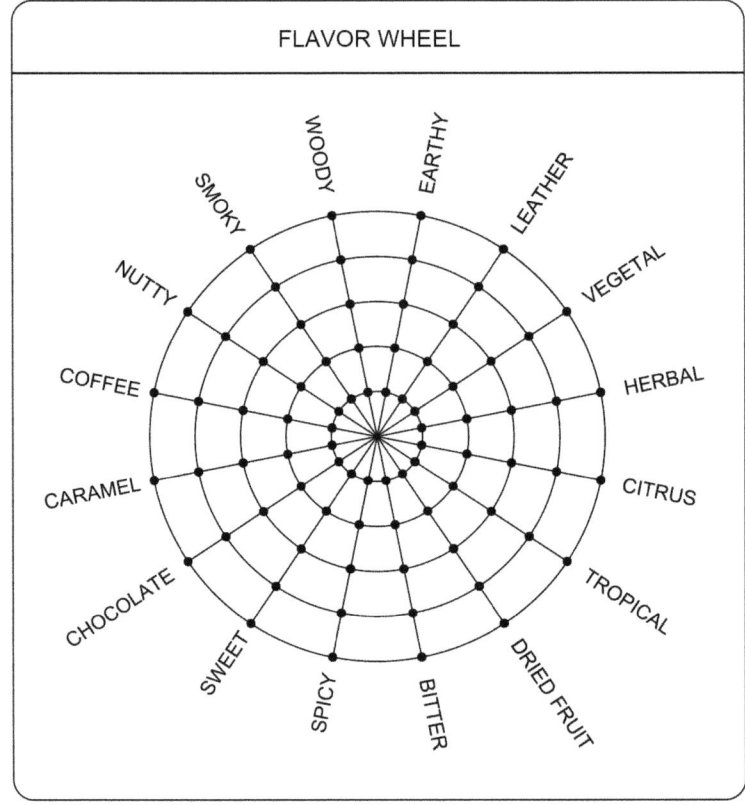

ADDITIONAL NOTES

FINAL RATING

- APPEARANCE ☆☆☆☆☆
- TASTE ☆☆☆☆☆
- MOUTHFEEL ☆☆☆☆☆
- OVERALL RATING ☆☆☆☆☆

	NAME		
	DISTILLERY		TYPE
	ORIGIN		AGE
	PRICE		SAMPLED

COLOR METER

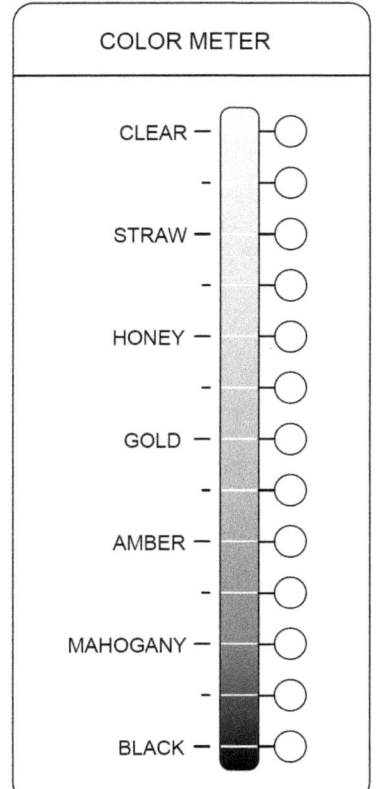

- CLEAR
- STRAW
- HONEY
- GOLD
- AMBER
- MAHOGANY
- BLACK

FLAVOR WHEEL

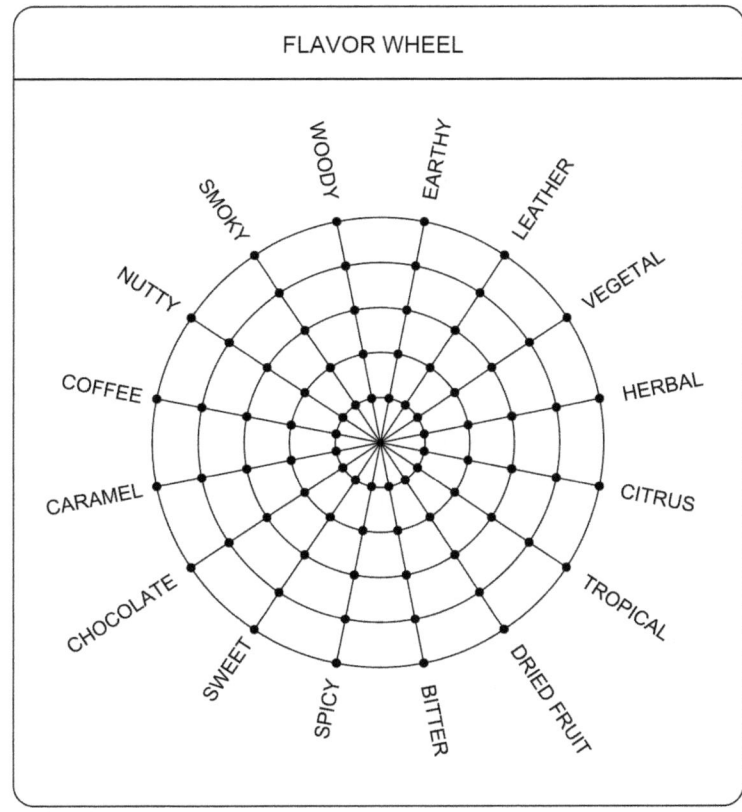

SMOKY · WOODY · EARTHY · LEATHER · VEGETAL · HERBAL · CITRUS · TROPICAL · DRIED FRUIT · BITTER · SPICY · SWEET · CHOCOLATE · CARAMEL · COFFEE · NUTTY

ADDITIONAL NOTES

FINAL RATING

- APPEARANCE ☆☆☆☆☆
- TASTE ☆☆☆☆☆
- MOUTHFEEL ☆☆☆☆☆
- OVERALL RATING ☆☆☆☆☆

	NAME		
	DISTILLERY		TYPE
	ORIGIN		AGE
	PRICE		SAMPLED

COLOR METER

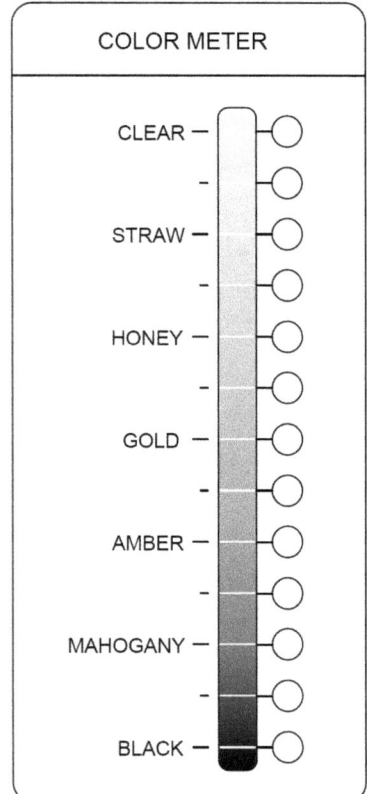

- CLEAR
- STRAW
- HONEY
- GOLD
- AMBER
- MAHOGANY
- BLACK

FLAVOR WHEEL

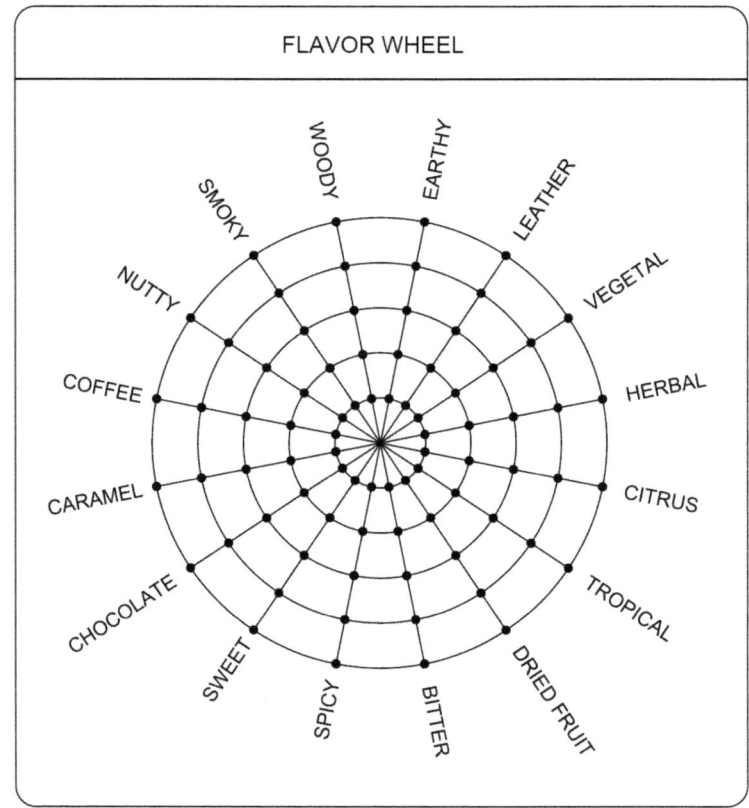

SMOKY, WOODY, EARTHY, LEATHER, NUTTY, VEGETAL, COFFEE, HERBAL, CARAMEL, CITRUS, CHOCOLATE, TROPICAL, SWEET, SPICY, BITTER, DRIED FRUIT

ADDITIONAL NOTES

FINAL RATING

- APPEARANCE ☆☆☆☆☆
- TASTE ☆☆☆☆☆
- MOUTHFEEL ☆☆☆☆☆
- OVERALL RATING ☆☆☆☆☆

	NAME		
	DISTILLERY		TYPE
	ORIGIN		AGE
	PRICE		SAMPLED

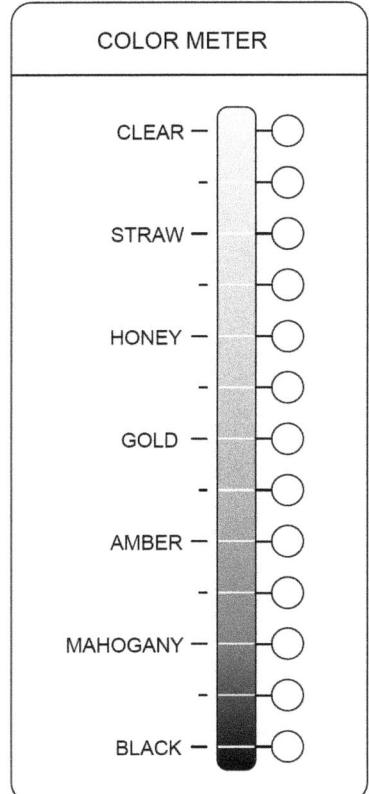

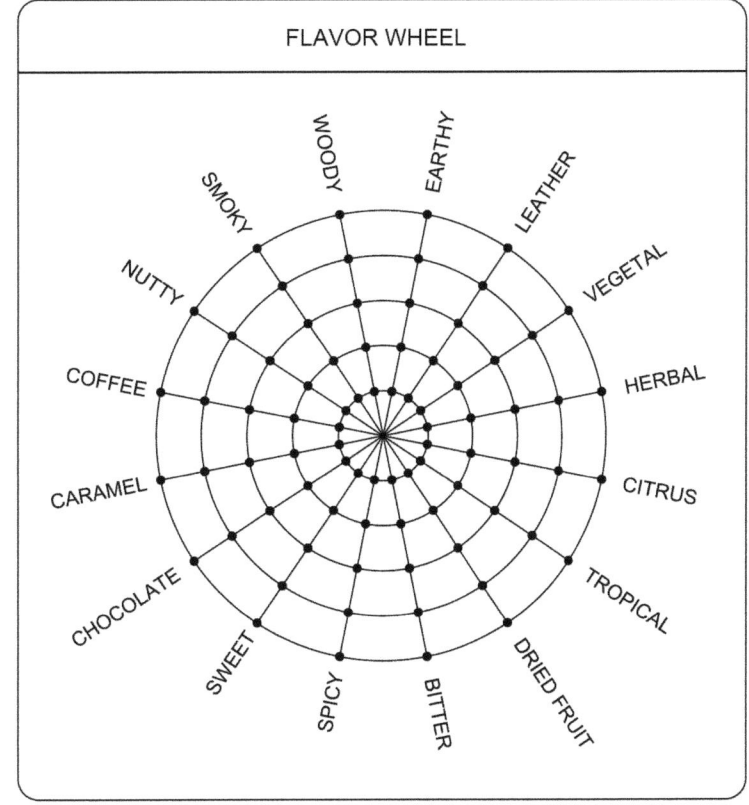

ADDITIONAL NOTES

FINAL RATING

- APPEARANCE ☆☆☆☆☆
- TASTE ☆☆☆☆☆
- MOUTHFEEL ☆☆☆☆☆
- OVERALL RATING ☆☆☆☆☆

	NAME		
	DISTILLERY		TYPE
	ORIGIN		AGE
	PRICE		SAMPLED

COLOR METER

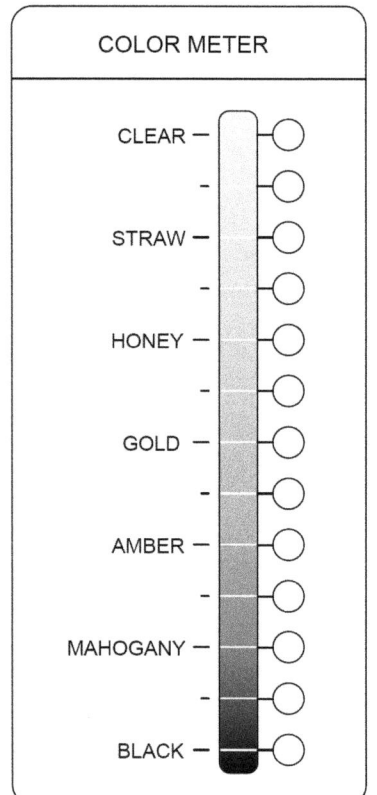

- CLEAR
- STRAW
- HONEY
- GOLD
- AMBER
- MAHOGANY
- BLACK

FLAVOR WHEEL

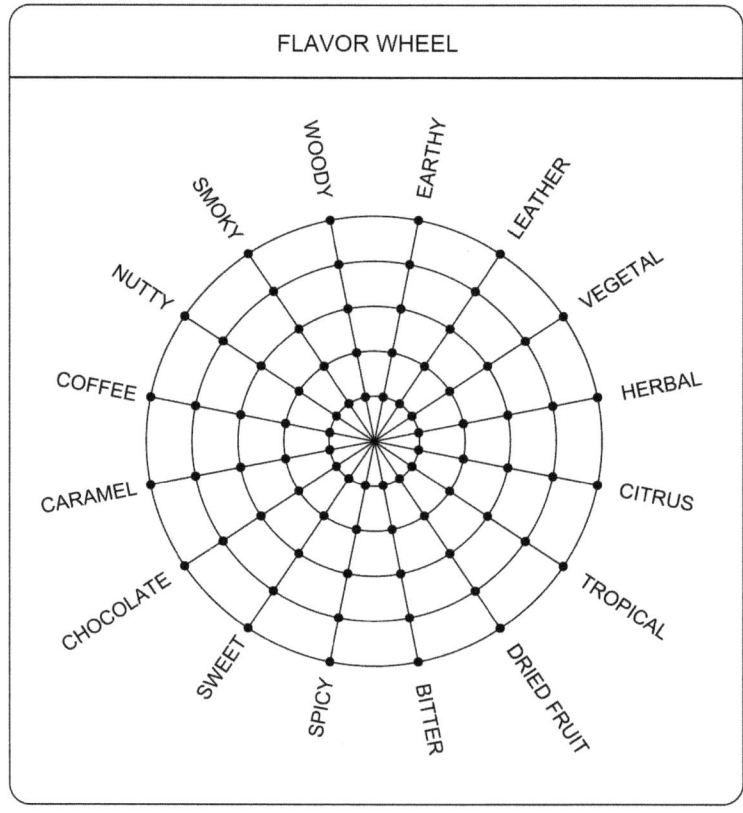

SMOKY, WOODY, EARTHY, LEATHER, VEGETAL, HERBAL, CITRUS, TROPICAL, DRIED FRUIT, BITTER, SPICY, SWEET, CHOCOLATE, CARAMEL, COFFEE, NUTTY

ADDITIONAL NOTES

FINAL RATING

- APPEARANCE ☆☆☆☆☆
- TASTE ☆☆☆☆☆
- MOUTHFEEL ☆☆☆☆☆
- OVERALL RATING ☆☆☆☆☆

	NAME		
	DISTILLERY		TYPE
	ORIGIN		AGE
	PRICE		SAMPLED

COLOR METER

- CLEAR
- STRAW
- HONEY
- GOLD
- AMBER
- MAHOGANY
- BLACK

FLAVOR WHEEL

SMOKY, WOODY, EARTHY, LEATHER, VEGETAL, HERBAL, CITRUS, TROPICAL, DRIED FRUIT, BITTER, SPICY, SWEET, CHOCOLATE, CARAMEL, COFFEE, NUTTY

ADDITIONAL NOTES

FINAL RATING

- APPEARANCE ☆☆☆☆☆
- TASTE ☆☆☆☆☆
- MOUTHFEEL ☆☆☆☆☆
- OVERALL RATING ☆☆☆☆☆

	NAME		
	DISTILLERY		TYPE
	ORIGIN		AGE
	PRICE		SAMPLED

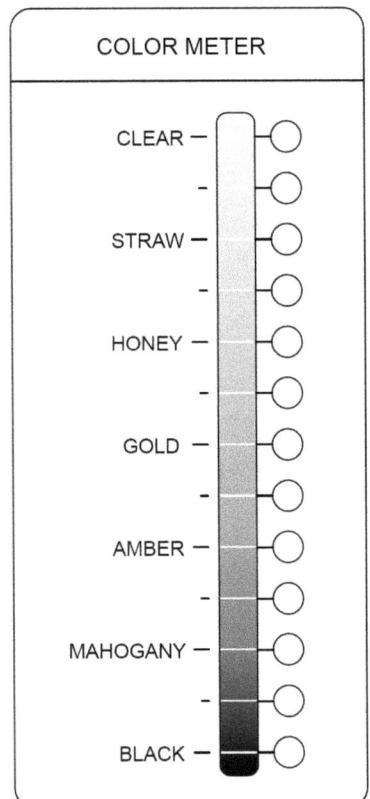

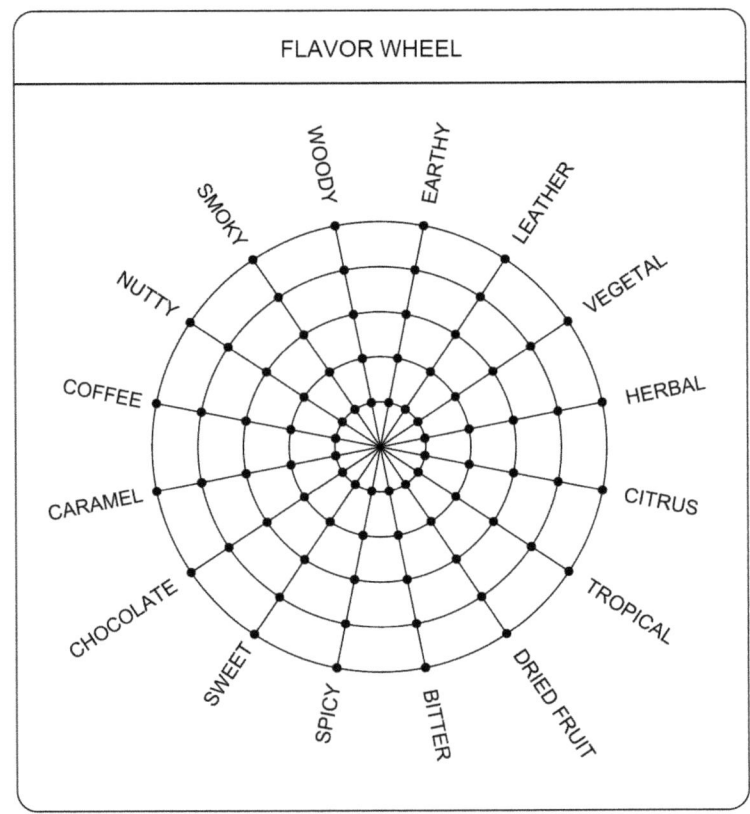

ADDITIONAL NOTES

FINAL RATING

- APPEARANCE ☆☆☆☆☆
- TASTE ☆☆☆☆☆
- MOUTHFEEL ☆☆☆☆☆
- OVERALL RATING ☆☆☆☆☆

NAME	
DISTILLERY	TYPE
ORIGIN	AGE
PRICE	SAMPLED

COLOR METER

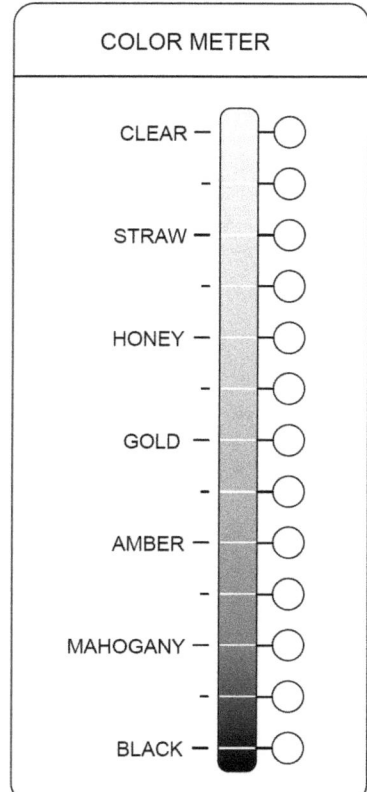

- CLEAR
- STRAW
- HONEY
- GOLD
- AMBER
- MAHOGANY
- BLACK

FLAVOR WHEEL

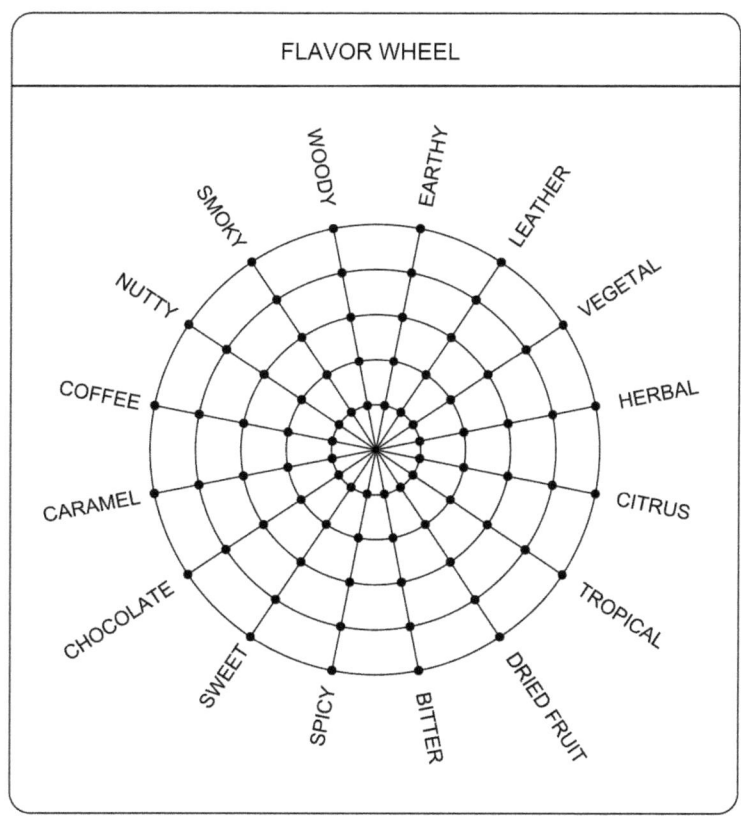

SMOKY, WOODY, EARTHY, LEATHER, VEGETAL, HERBAL, CITRUS, TROPICAL, DRIED FRUIT, BITTER, SPICY, SWEET, CHOCOLATE, CARAMEL, COFFEE, NUTTY

ADDITIONAL NOTES

FINAL RATING

- APPEARANCE ☆☆☆☆☆
- TASTE ☆☆☆☆☆
- MOUTHFEEL ☆☆☆☆☆
- OVERALL RATING ☆☆☆☆☆

NAME			
DISTILLERY		TYPE	
ORIGIN		AGE	
PRICE		SAMPLED	

COLOR METER

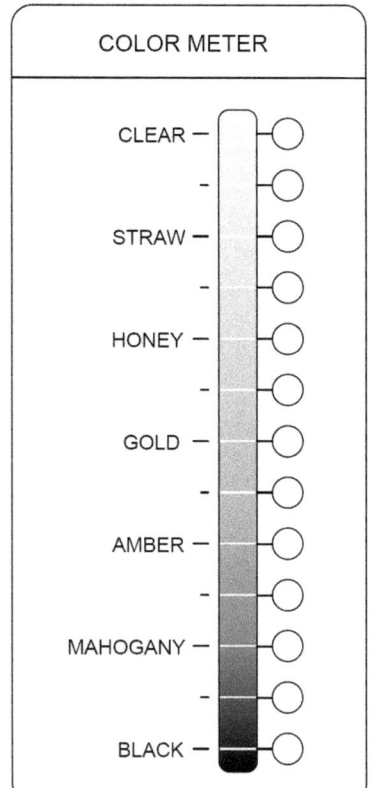

- CLEAR
- STRAW
- HONEY
- GOLD
- AMBER
- MAHOGANY
- BLACK

FLAVOR WHEEL

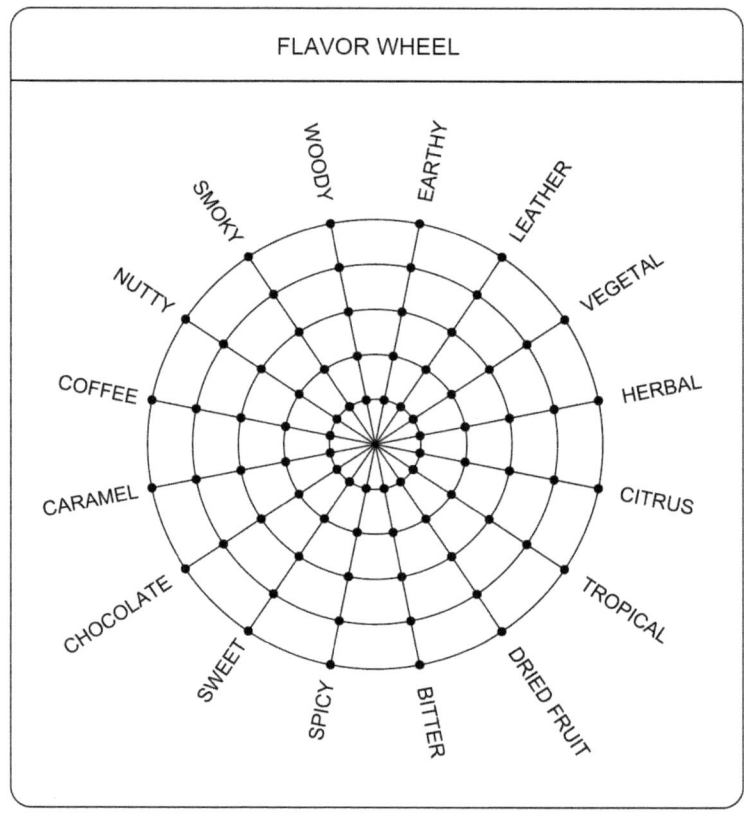

SMOKY, WOODY, EARTHY, LEATHER, VEGETAL, HERBAL, CITRUS, TROPICAL, DRIED FRUIT, BITTER, SPICY, SWEET, CHOCOLATE, CARAMEL, COFFEE, NUTTY

ADDITIONAL NOTES

FINAL RATING

- APPEARANCE ☆☆☆☆☆
- TASTE ☆☆☆☆☆
- MOUTHFEEL ☆☆☆☆☆
- OVERALL RATING ☆☆☆☆☆

🥃 NAME			
🛢️ DISTILLERY		🍾 TYPE	
🌍 ORIGIN		🛢️ AGE	
💰 PRICE		📅 SAMPLED	

COLOR METER

- CLEAR
- STRAW
- HONEY
- GOLD
- AMBER
- MAHOGANY
- BLACK

FLAVOR WHEEL

WOODY, EARTHY, LEATHER, VEGETAL, HERBAL, CITRUS, TROPICAL, DRIED FRUIT, BITTER, SPICY, SWEET, CHOCOLATE, CARAMEL, COFFEE, NUTTY, SMOKY

ADDITIONAL NOTES

FINAL RATING

- APPEARANCE ☆☆☆☆☆
- TASTE ☆☆☆☆☆
- MOUTHFEEL ☆☆☆☆☆
- OVERALL RATING ☆☆☆☆☆

🥃 NAME			
🏭 DISTILLERY		🍾 TYPE	
🌍 ORIGIN		🛢 AGE	
💰 PRICE		📅 SAMPLED	

COLOR METER

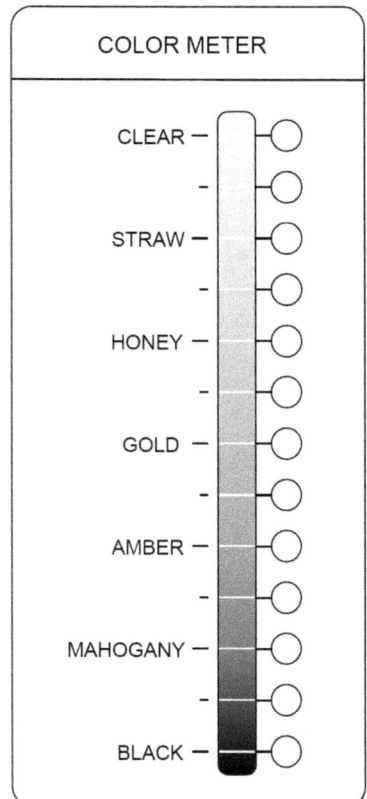

- CLEAR
- STRAW
- HONEY
- GOLD
- AMBER
- MAHOGANY
- BLACK

FLAVOR WHEEL

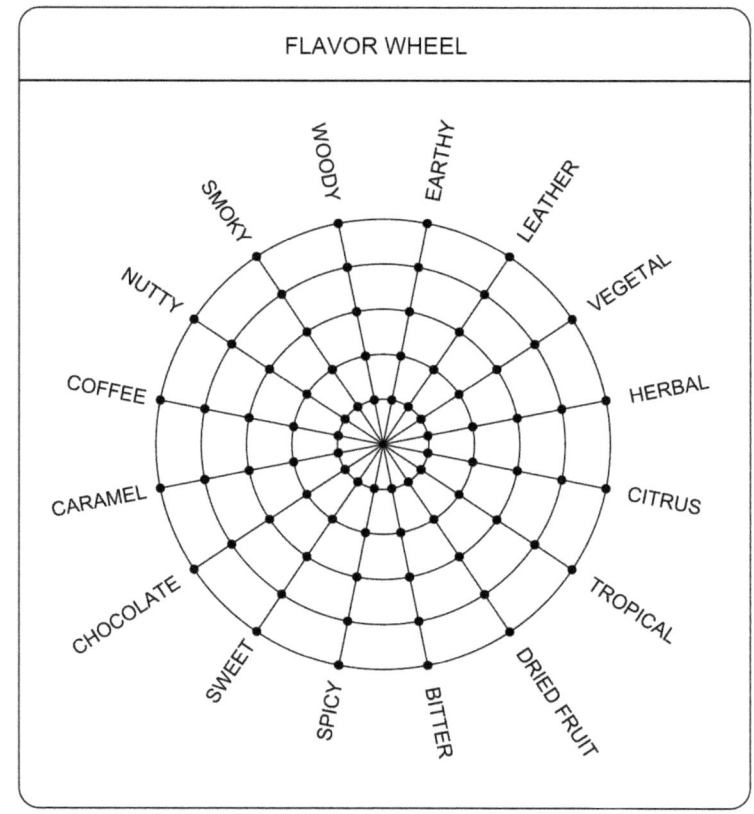

WOODY, EARTHY, LEATHER, VEGETAL, HERBAL, CITRUS, TROPICAL, DRIED FRUIT, BITTER, SPICY, SWEET, CHOCOLATE, CARAMEL, COFFEE, NUTTY, SMOKY

ADDITIONAL NOTES

FINAL RATING

- APPEARANCE ☆☆☆☆☆
- TASTE ☆☆☆☆☆
- MOUTHFEEL ☆☆☆☆☆
- OVERALL RATING ☆☆☆☆☆

	NAME		
	DISTILLERY		TYPE
	ORIGIN		AGE
	PRICE		SAMPLED

COLOR METER

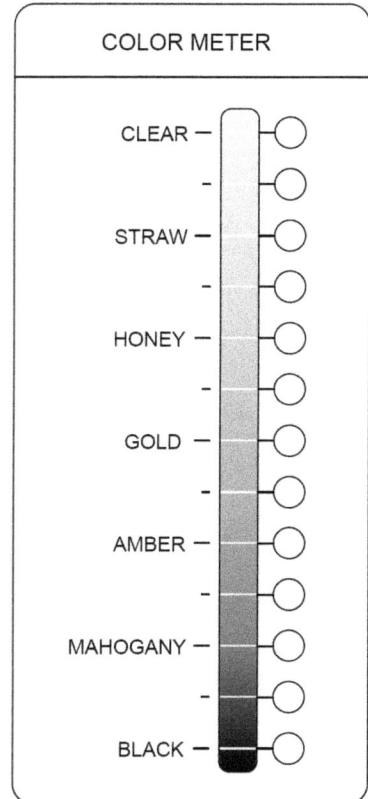

- CLEAR
- STRAW
- HONEY
- GOLD
- AMBER
- MAHOGANY
- BLACK

FLAVOR WHEEL

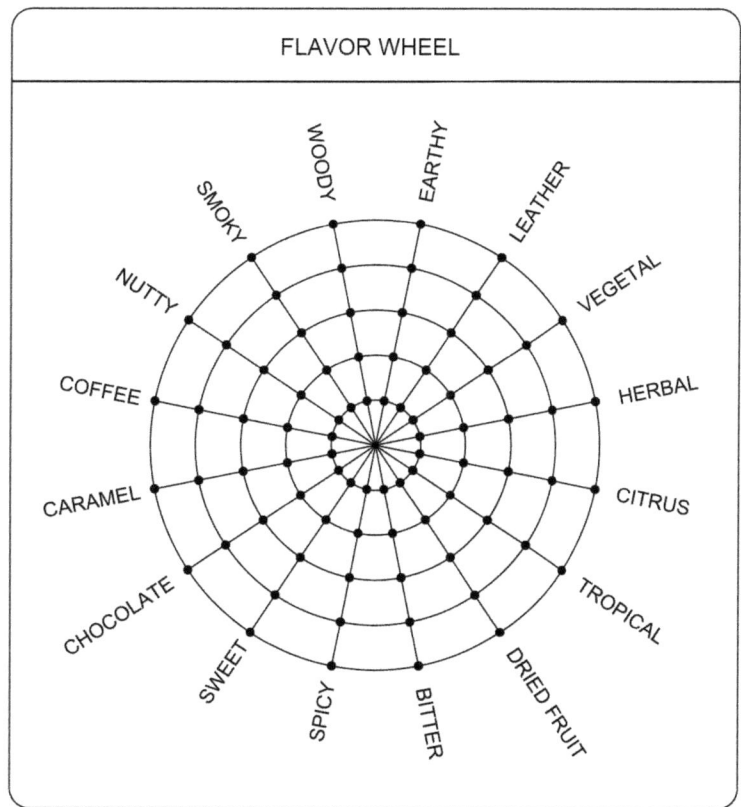

SMOKY, WOODY, EARTHY, LEATHER, NUTTY, VEGETAL, COFFEE, HERBAL, CARAMEL, CITRUS, CHOCOLATE, TROPICAL, SWEET, SPICY, BITTER, DRIED FRUIT

ADDITIONAL NOTES

FINAL RATING

- APPEARANCE ☆☆☆☆☆
- TASTE ☆☆☆☆☆
- MOUTHFEEL ☆☆☆☆☆
- OVERALL RATING ☆☆☆☆☆

	NAME		
	DISTILLERY		TYPE
	ORIGIN		AGE
	PRICE		SAMPLED

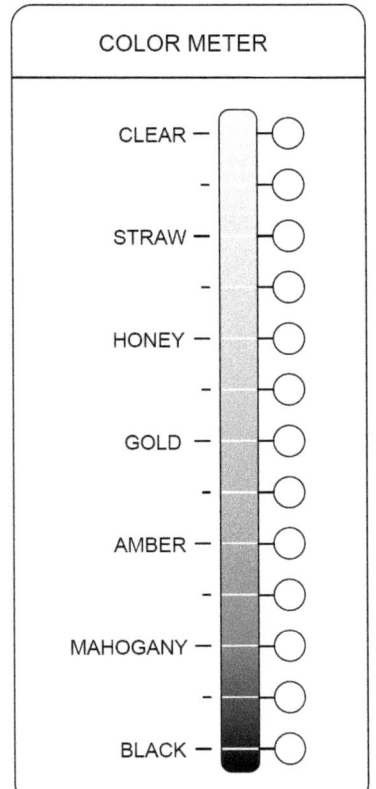

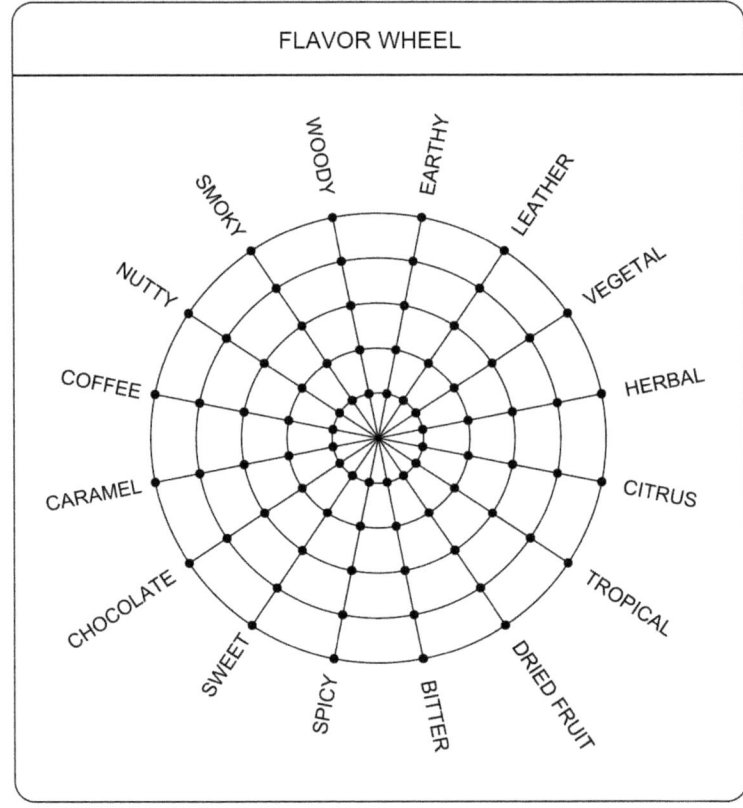

ADDITIONAL NOTES

FINAL RATING

- APPEARANCE ☆☆☆☆☆
- TASTE ☆☆☆☆☆
- MOUTHFEEL ☆☆☆☆☆
- OVERALL RATING ☆☆☆☆☆

NAME			
DISTILLERY		TYPE	
ORIGIN		AGE	
PRICE		SAMPLED	

COLOR METER

- CLEAR
- STRAW
- HONEY
- GOLD
- AMBER
- MAHOGANY
- BLACK

FLAVOR WHEEL

WOODY, EARTHY, LEATHER, VEGETAL, HERBAL, CITRUS, TROPICAL, DRIED FRUIT, BITTER, SPICY, SWEET, CHOCOLATE, CARAMEL, COFFEE, NUTTY, SMOKY

ADDITIONAL NOTES

FINAL RATING

- APPEARANCE ☆☆☆☆☆
- TASTE ☆☆☆☆☆
- MOUTHFEEL ☆☆☆☆☆
- OVERALL RATING ☆☆☆☆☆

🥃 NAME			
🛢️ DISTILLERY		🍾 TYPE	
🌍 ORIGIN		🛢️ AGE	
💵 PRICE		📅 SAMPLED	

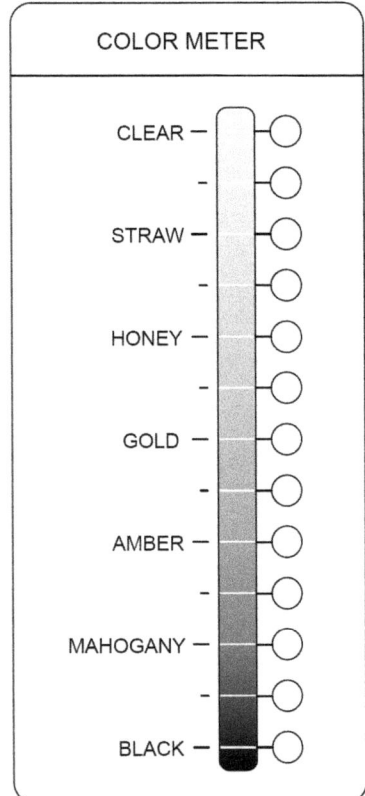

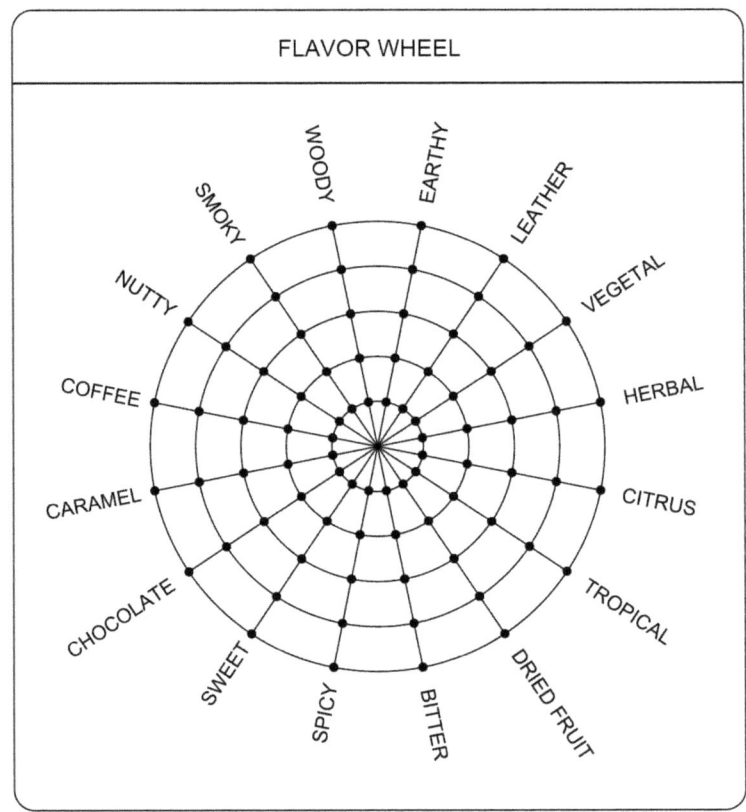

ADDITIONAL NOTES

FINAL RATING

🍾 APPEARANCE ☆☆☆☆☆

🌾 TASTE ☆☆☆☆☆

👄 MOUTHFEEL ☆☆☆☆☆

⭐ OVERALL RATING ☆☆☆☆☆

NAME			
DISTILLERY		TYPE	
ORIGIN		AGE	
PRICE		SAMPLED	

COLOR METER

- CLEAR
- STRAW
- HONEY
- GOLD
- AMBER
- MAHOGANY
- BLACK

FLAVOR WHEEL

SMOKY, WOODY, EARTHY, LEATHER, VEGETAL, HERBAL, CITRUS, TROPICAL, DRIED FRUIT, BITTER, SPICY, SWEET, CHOCOLATE, CARAMEL, COFFEE, NUTTY

ADDITIONAL NOTES

FINAL RATING

- APPEARANCE ☆☆☆☆☆
- TASTE ☆☆☆☆☆
- MOUTHFEEL ☆☆☆☆☆
- OVERALL RATING ☆☆☆☆☆

	NAME		
	DISTILLERY		TYPE
	ORIGIN		AGE
	PRICE		SAMPLED

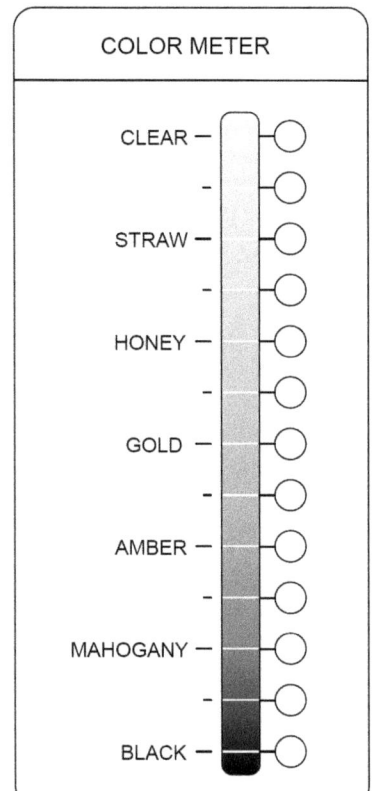

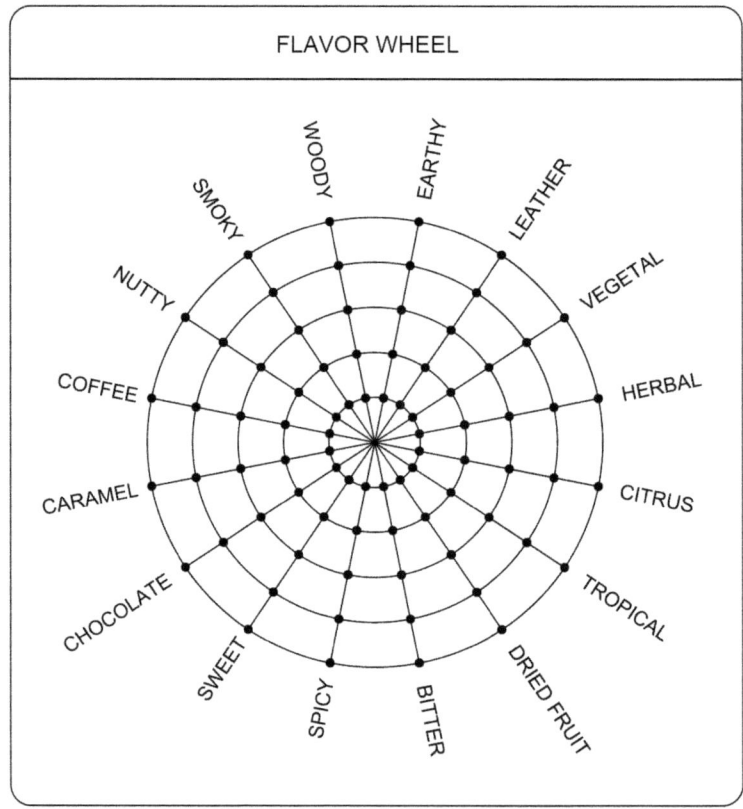

ADDITIONAL NOTES

FINAL RATING

- APPEARANCE ☆☆☆☆☆
- TASTE ☆☆☆☆☆
- MOUTHFEEL ☆☆☆☆☆
- OVERALL RATING ☆☆☆☆☆

	NAME		
	DISTILLERY		TYPE
	ORIGIN		AGE
	PRICE		SAMPLED

COLOR METER

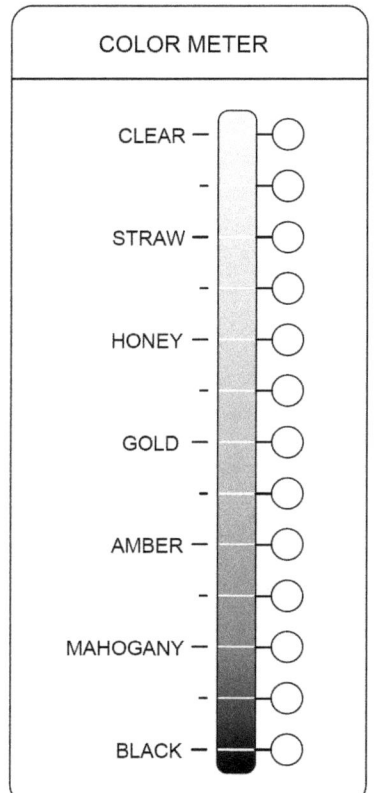

- CLEAR
- STRAW
- HONEY
- GOLD
- AMBER
- MAHOGANY
- BLACK

FLAVOR WHEEL

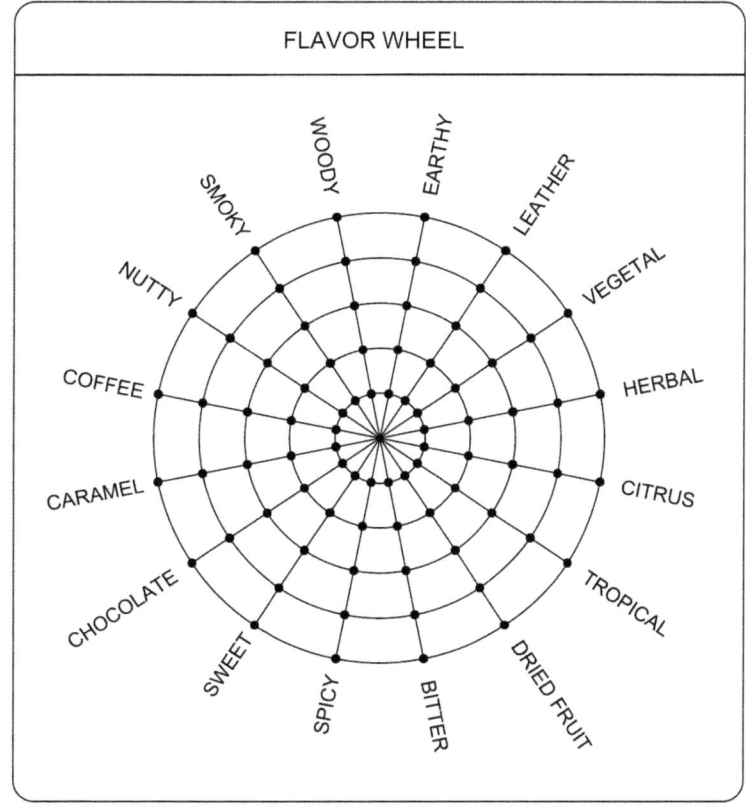

SMOKY, WOODY, EARTHY, LEATHER, NUTTY, VEGETAL, COFFEE, HERBAL, CARAMEL, CITRUS, CHOCOLATE, TROPICAL, SWEET, SPICY, BITTER, DRIED FRUIT

ADDITIONAL NOTES

FINAL RATING

- APPEARANCE ☆☆☆☆☆
- TASTE ☆☆☆☆☆
- MOUTHFEEL ☆☆☆☆☆
- OVERALL RATING ☆☆☆☆☆

	NAME		
	DISTILLERY		TYPE
	ORIGIN		AGE
	PRICE		SAMPLED

COLOR METER

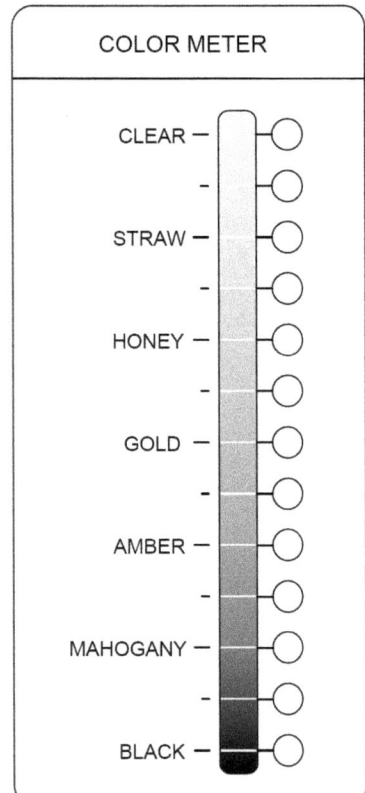

- CLEAR
- STRAW
- HONEY
- GOLD
- AMBER
- MAHOGANY
- BLACK

FLAVOR WHEEL

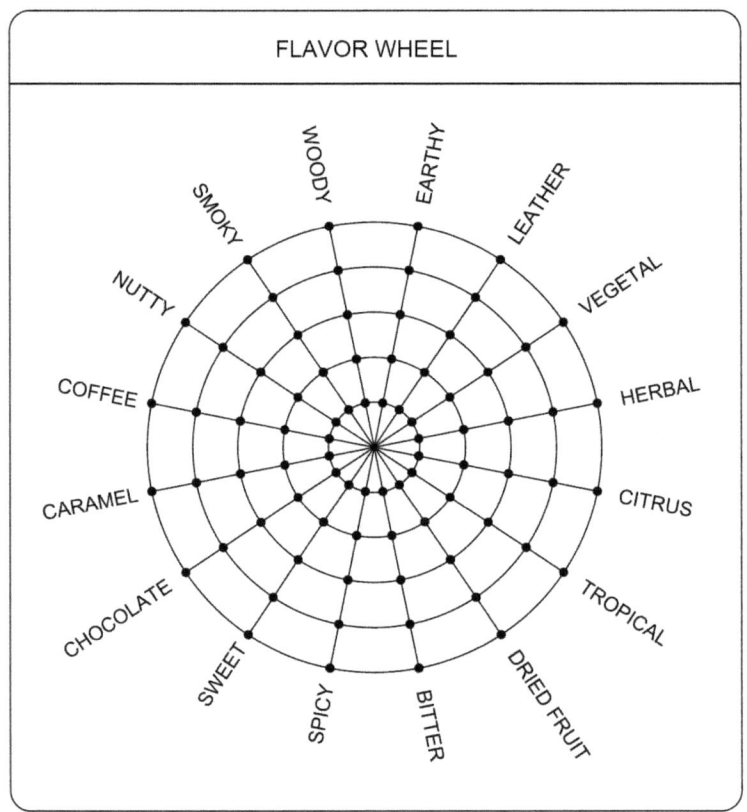

SMOKY, WOODY, EARTHY, LEATHER, VEGETAL, HERBAL, CITRUS, TROPICAL, DRIED FRUIT, BITTER, SPICY, SWEET, CHOCOLATE, CARAMEL, COFFEE, NUTTY

ADDITIONAL NOTES

FINAL RATING

- APPEARANCE ☆☆☆☆☆
- TASTE ☆☆☆☆☆
- MOUTHFEEL ☆☆☆☆☆
- OVERALL RATING ☆☆☆☆☆

	NAME		
	DISTILLERY		TYPE
	ORIGIN		AGE
	PRICE		SAMPLED

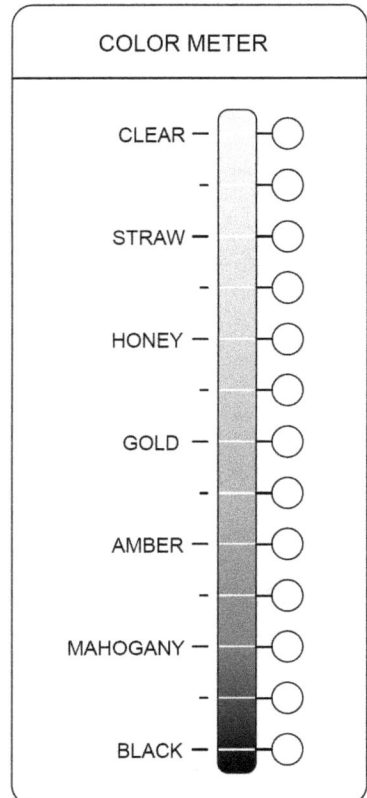

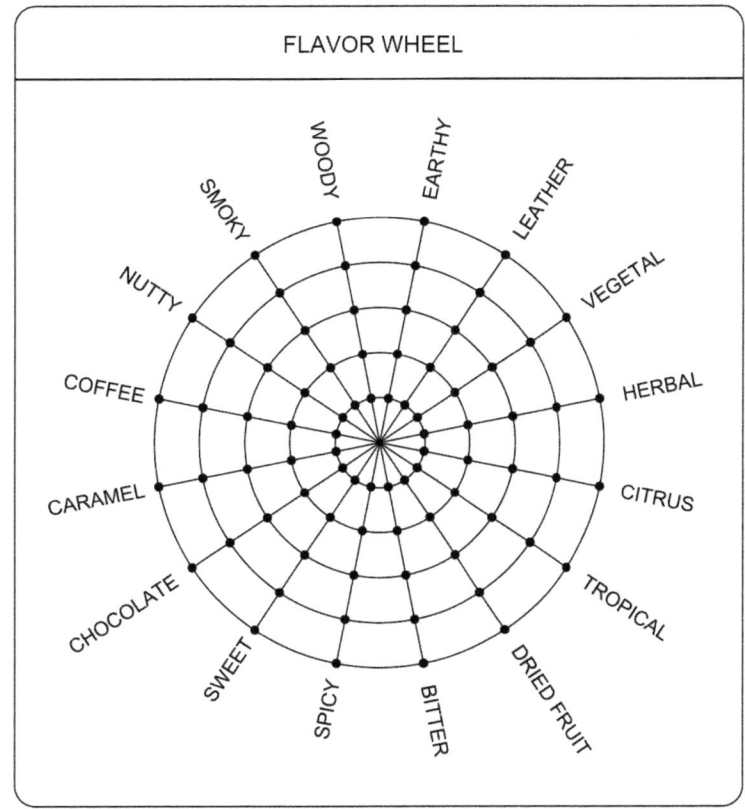

ADDITIONAL NOTES

FINAL RATING

- APPEARANCE ☆☆☆☆☆
- TASTE ☆☆☆☆☆
- MOUTHFEEL ☆☆☆☆☆
- OVERALL RATING ☆☆☆☆☆

NAME			
DISTILLERY		TYPE	
ORIGIN		AGE	
PRICE		SAMPLED	

COLOR METER

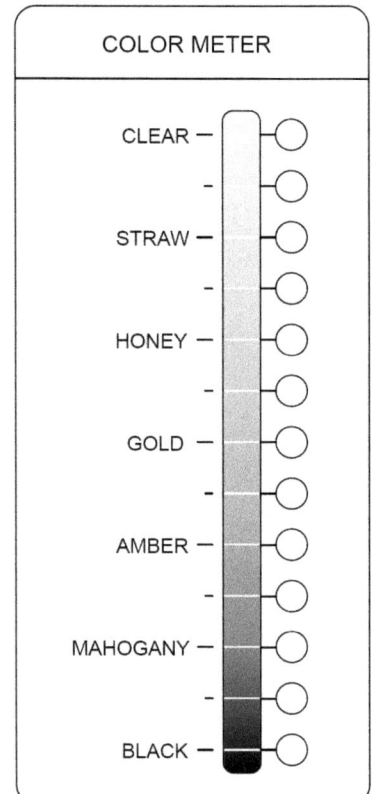

- CLEAR
- STRAW
- HONEY
- GOLD
- AMBER
- MAHOGANY
- BLACK

FLAVOR WHEEL

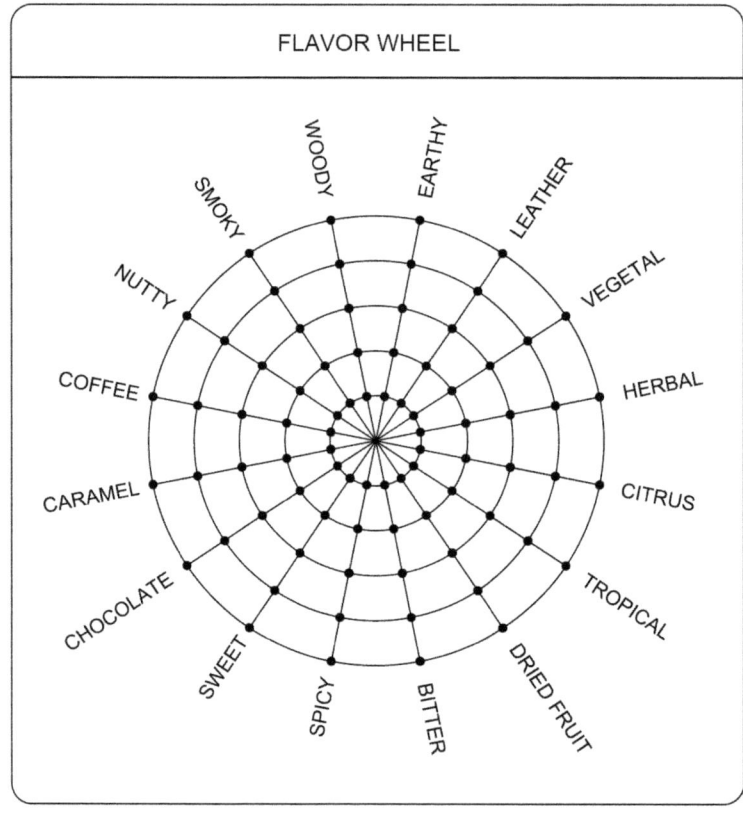

SMOKY, WOODY, EARTHY, LEATHER, NUTTY, VEGETAL, COFFEE, HERBAL, CARAMEL, CITRUS, CHOCOLATE, TROPICAL, SWEET, SPICY, BITTER, DRIED FRUIT

ADDITIONAL NOTES

FINAL RATING

- APPEARANCE ☆☆☆☆☆
- TASTE ☆☆☆☆☆
- MOUTHFEEL ☆☆☆☆☆
- OVERALL RATING ☆☆☆☆☆

	NAME		
	DISTILLERY		TYPE
	ORIGIN		AGE
	PRICE		SAMPLED

COLOR METER

- CLEAR
- STRAW
- HONEY
- GOLD
- AMBER
- MAHOGANY
- BLACK

FLAVOR WHEEL

SMOKY, WOODY, EARTHY, LEATHER, VEGETAL, HERBAL, CITRUS, TROPICAL, DRIED FRUIT, BITTER, SPICY, SWEET, CHOCOLATE, CARAMEL, COFFEE, NUTTY

ADDITIONAL NOTES

FINAL RATING

- APPEARANCE ☆☆☆☆☆
- TASTE ☆☆☆☆☆
- MOUTHFEEL ☆☆☆☆☆
- OVERALL RATING ☆☆☆☆☆

	NAME		
	DISTILLERY		TYPE
	ORIGIN		AGE
	PRICE		SAMPLED

COLOR METER

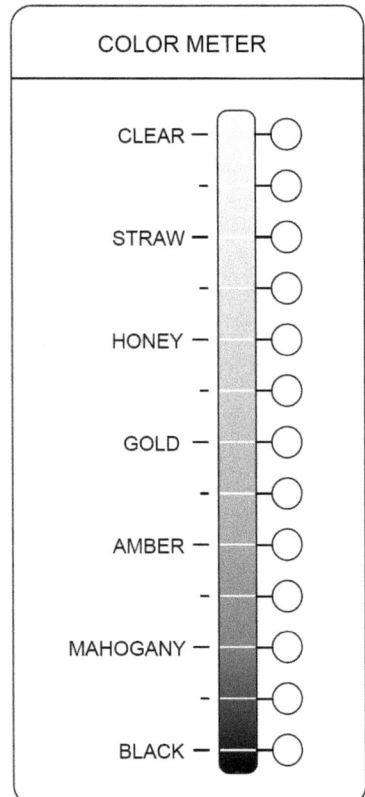

- CLEAR
- STRAW
- HONEY
- GOLD
- AMBER
- MAHOGANY
- BLACK

FLAVOR WHEEL

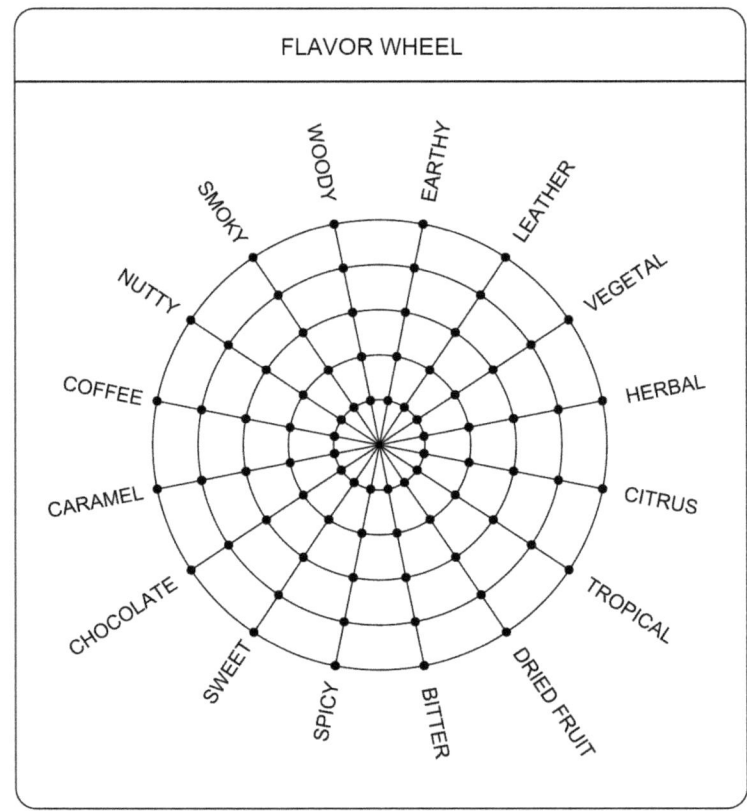

SMOKY, WOODY, EARTHY, LEATHER, NUTTY, VEGETAL, COFFEE, HERBAL, CARAMEL, CITRUS, CHOCOLATE, TROPICAL, SWEET, SPICY, BITTER, DRIED FRUIT

ADDITIONAL NOTES

FINAL RATING

- APPEARANCE ☆☆☆☆☆
- TASTE ☆☆☆☆☆
- MOUTHFEEL ☆☆☆☆☆
- OVERALL RATING ☆☆☆☆☆

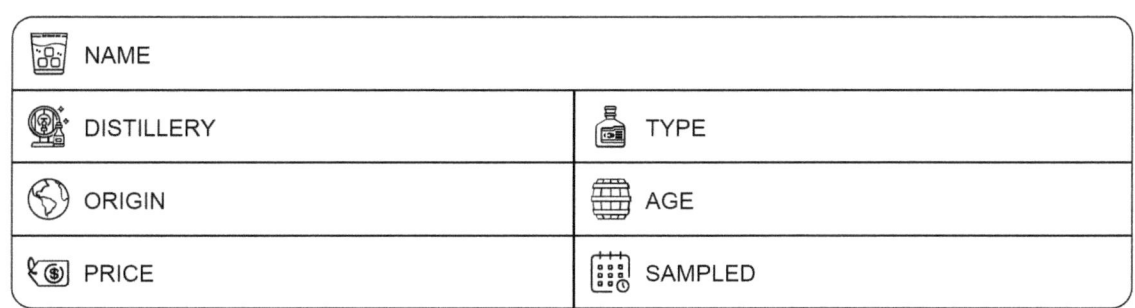

	NAME		
	DISTILLERY		TYPE
	ORIGIN		AGE
	PRICE		SAMPLED

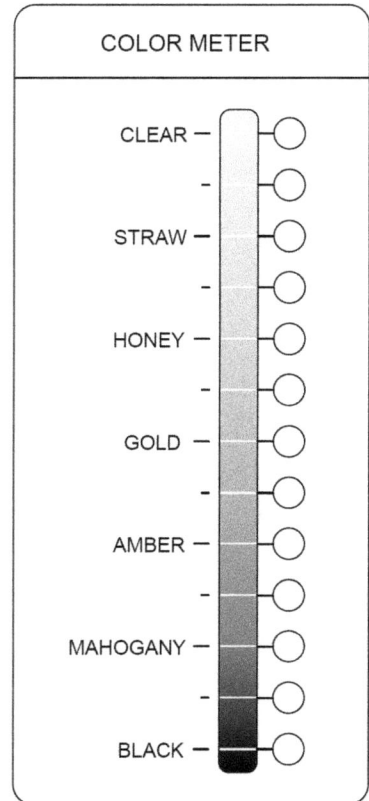

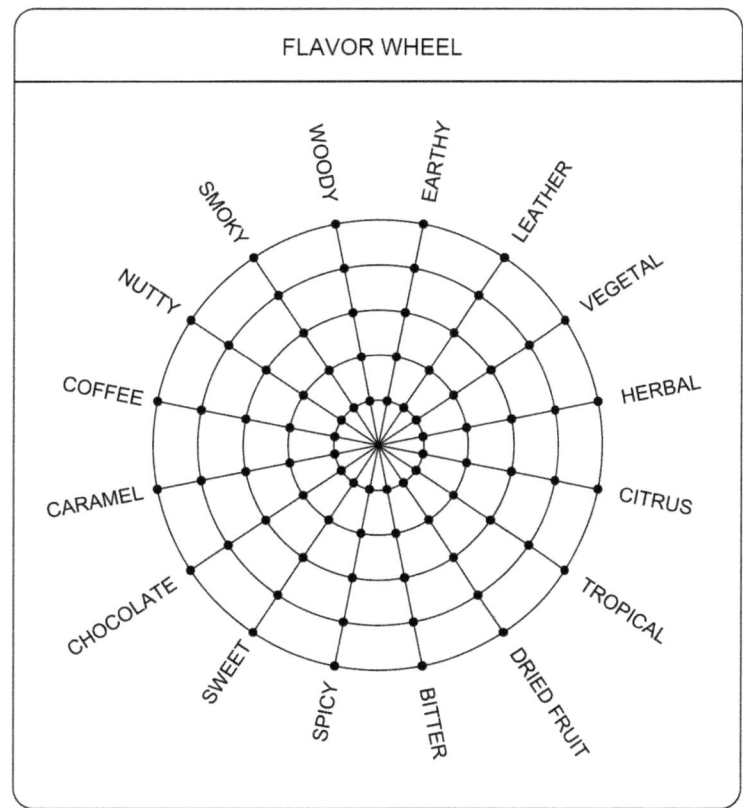

ADDITIONAL NOTES

FINAL RATING

- APPEARANCE ☆☆☆☆☆
- TASTE ☆☆☆☆☆
- MOUTHFEEL ☆☆☆☆☆
- OVERALL RATING ☆☆☆☆☆

	NAME		
	DISTILLERY		TYPE
	ORIGIN		AGE
	PRICE		SAMPLED

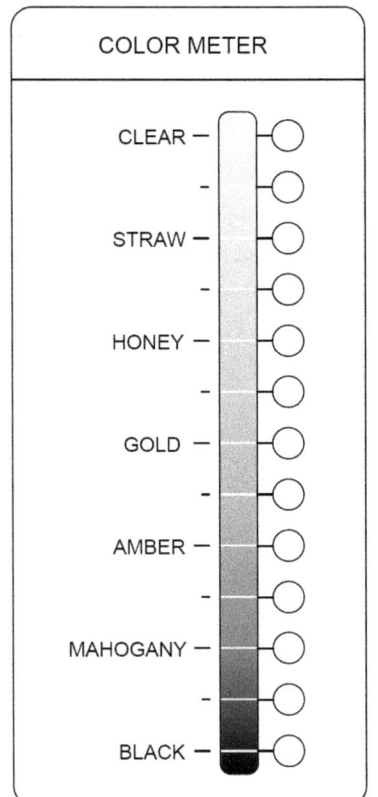

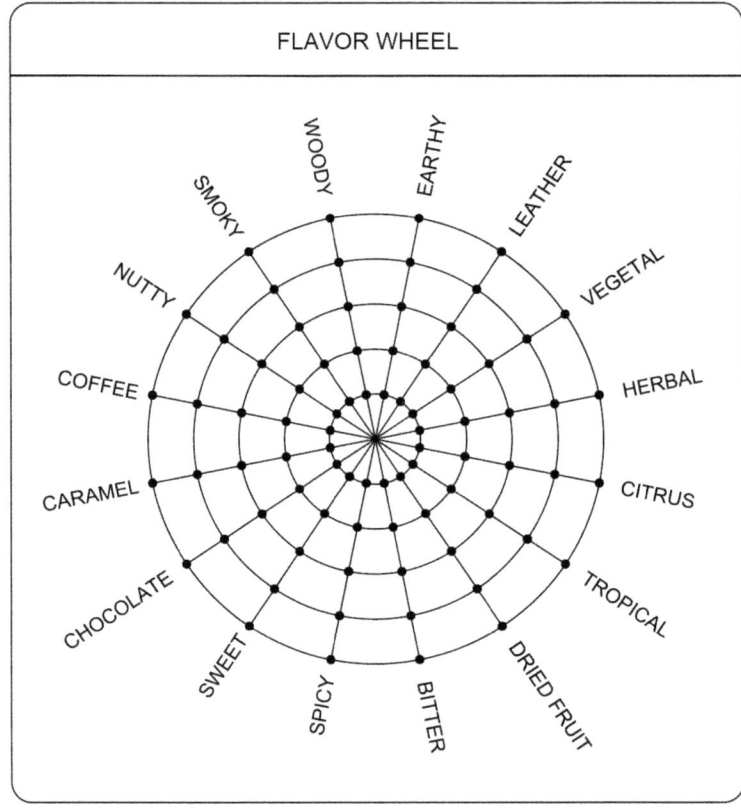

ADDITIONAL NOTES

FINAL RATING

- APPEARANCE ☆☆☆☆☆
- TASTE ☆☆☆☆☆
- MOUTHFEEL ☆☆☆☆☆
- OVERALL RATING ☆☆☆☆☆

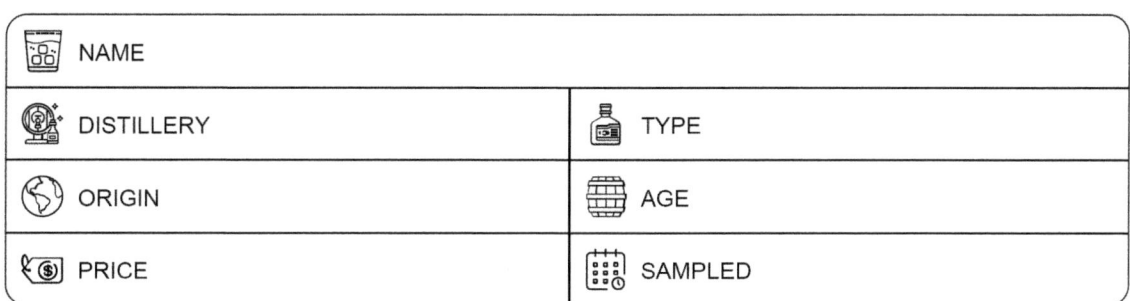

	NAME		
	DISTILLERY		TYPE
	ORIGIN		AGE
	PRICE		SAMPLED

COLOR METER

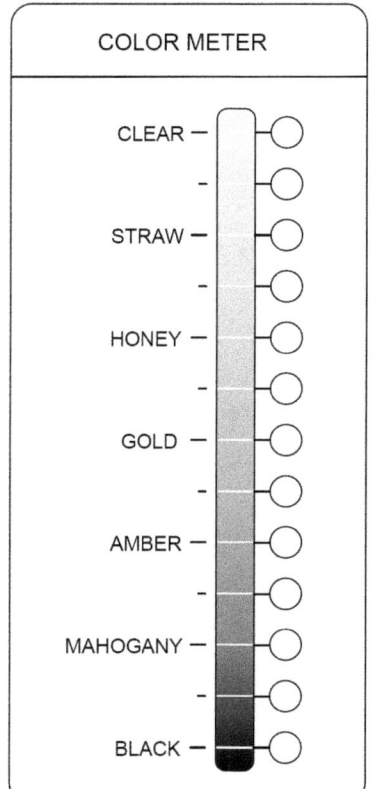

- CLEAR
- STRAW
- HONEY
- GOLD
- AMBER
- MAHOGANY
- BLACK

FLAVOR WHEEL

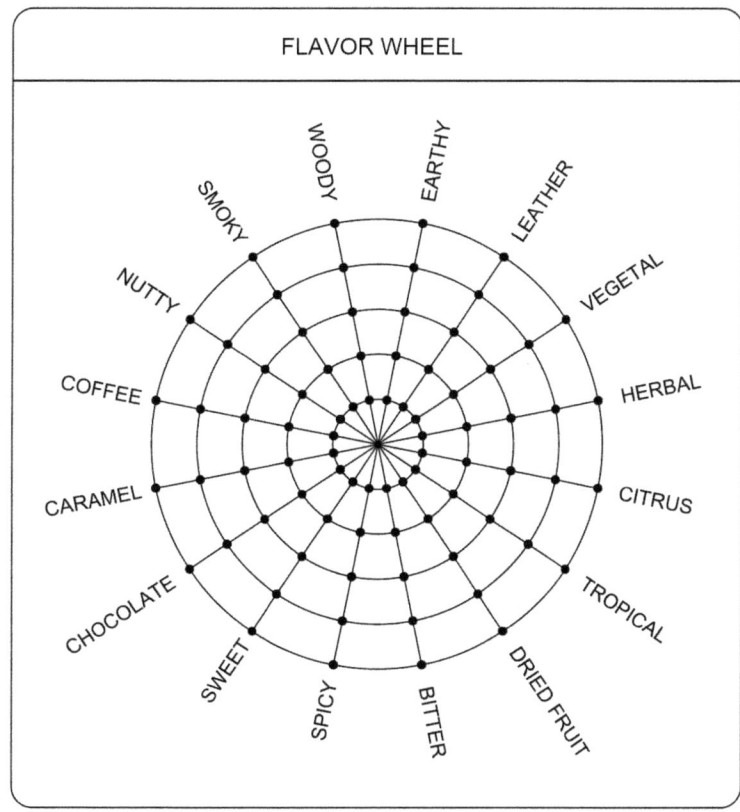

ADDITIONAL NOTES

FINAL RATING

- APPEARANCE ☆☆☆☆☆
- TASTE ☆☆☆☆☆
- MOUTHFEEL ☆☆☆☆☆
- OVERALL RATING ☆☆☆☆☆

🥃 NAME			
🏭 DISTILLERY		🍾 TYPE	
🌍 ORIGIN		🛢 AGE	
💲 PRICE		📅 SAMPLED	

COLOR METER

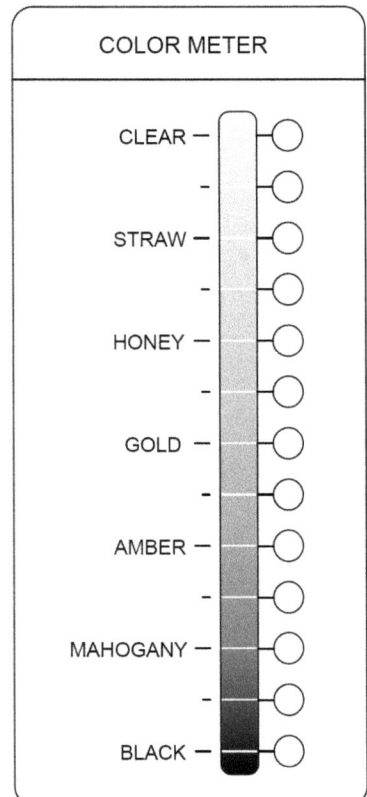

- CLEAR
- STRAW
- HONEY
- GOLD
- AMBER
- MAHOGANY
- BLACK

FLAVOR WHEEL

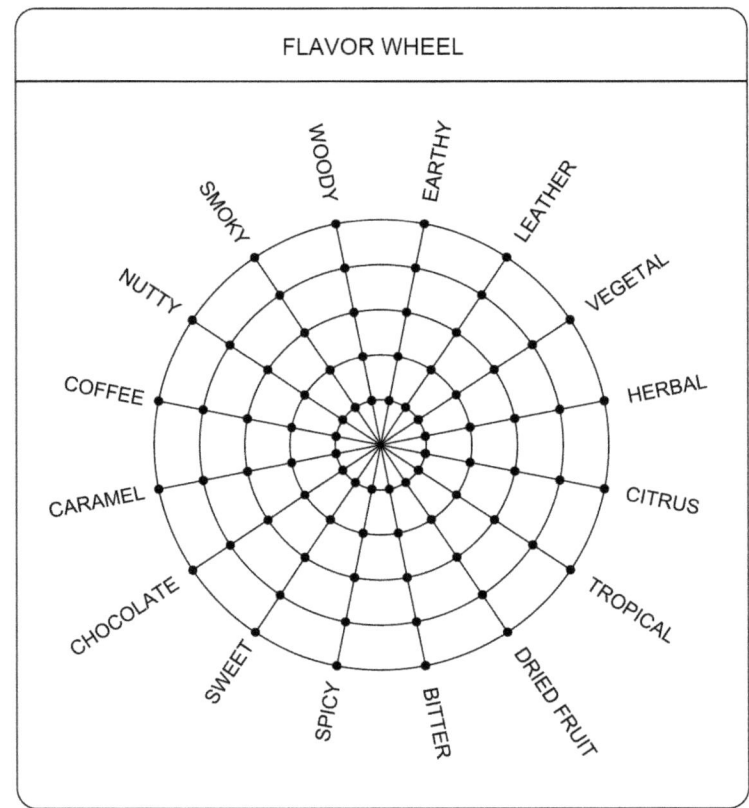

SMOKY, WOODY, EARTHY, LEATHER, VEGETAL, HERBAL, CITRUS, TROPICAL, DRIED FRUIT, BITTER, SPICY, SWEET, CHOCOLATE, CARAMEL, COFFEE, NUTTY

ADDITIONAL NOTES

FINAL RATING

- APPEARANCE ☆☆☆☆☆
- TASTE ☆☆☆☆☆
- MOUTHFEEL ☆☆☆☆☆
- OVERALL RATING ☆☆☆☆☆

🥃 NAME	
🛢️ DISTILLERY	🍾 TYPE
🌍 ORIGIN	🛢️ AGE
💰 PRICE	📅 SAMPLED

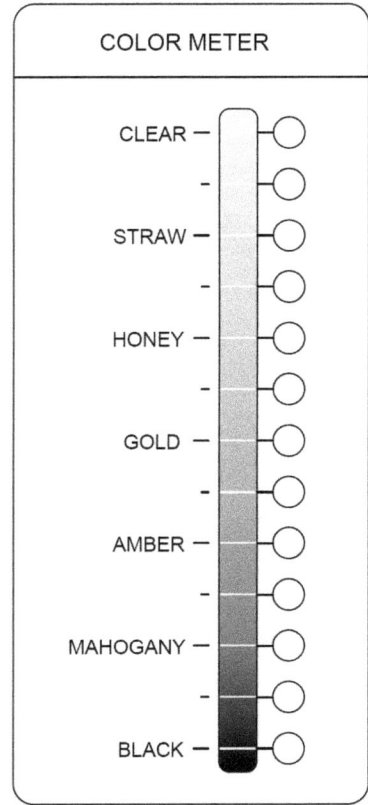

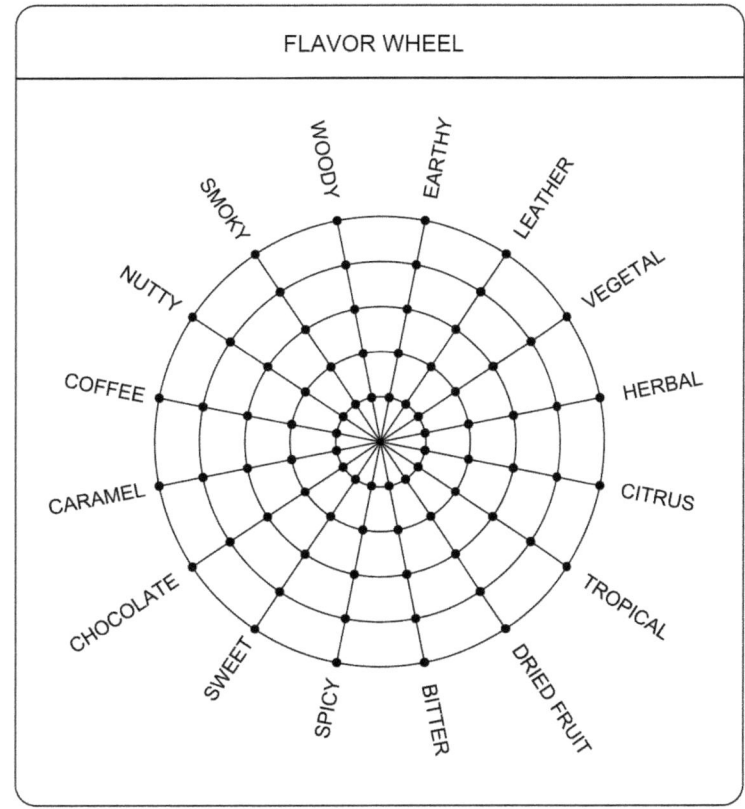

ADDITIONAL NOTES

FINAL RATING

- APPEARANCE ☆☆☆☆☆
- TASTE ☆☆☆☆☆
- MOUTHFEEL ☆☆☆☆☆
- OVERALL RATING ☆☆☆☆☆

	NAME		
	DISTILLERY		TYPE
	ORIGIN		AGE
	PRICE		SAMPLED

COLOR METER

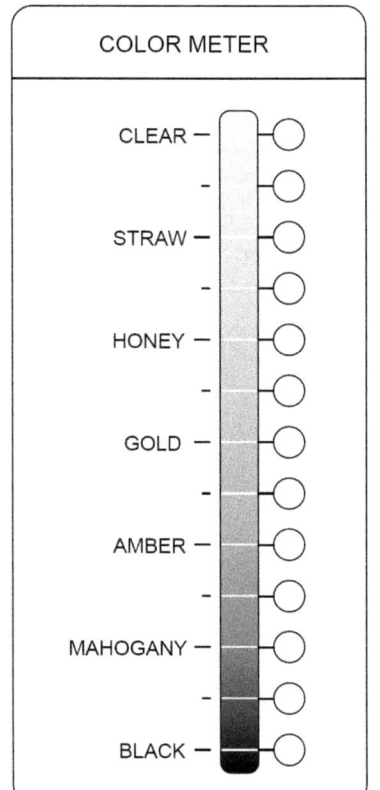

- CLEAR
- STRAW
- HONEY
- GOLD
- AMBER
- MAHOGANY
- BLACK

FLAVOR WHEEL

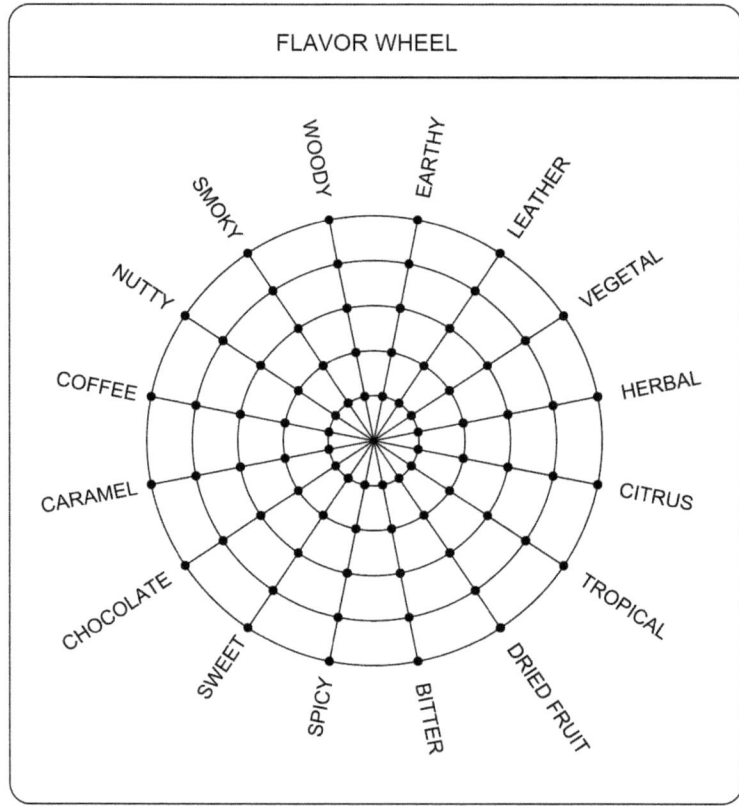

SMOKY, WOODY, EARTHY, LEATHER, VEGETAL, HERBAL, CITRUS, TROPICAL, DRIED FRUIT, BITTER, SPICY, SWEET, CHOCOLATE, CARAMEL, COFFEE, NUTTY

ADDITIONAL NOTES

FINAL RATING

- APPEARANCE ☆☆☆☆☆
- TASTE ☆☆☆☆☆
- MOUTHFEEL ☆☆☆☆☆
- OVERALL RATING ☆☆☆☆☆

	NAME		
	DISTILLERY		TYPE
	ORIGIN		AGE
	PRICE		SAMPLED

COLOR METER

- CLEAR
- STRAW
- HONEY
- GOLD
- AMBER
- MAHOGANY
- BLACK

FLAVOR WHEEL

WOODY, EARTHY, LEATHER, VEGETAL, HERBAL, CITRUS, TROPICAL, DRIED FRUIT, BITTER, SPICY, SWEET, CHOCOLATE, CARAMEL, COFFEE, NUTTY, SMOKY

ADDITIONAL NOTES

FINAL RATING

- APPEARANCE ☆☆☆☆☆
- TASTE ☆☆☆☆☆
- MOUTHFEEL ☆☆☆☆☆
- OVERALL RATING ☆☆☆☆☆

🥃 NAME			
⚙️ DISTILLERY		🍾 TYPE	
🌍 ORIGIN		🛢️ AGE	
💵 PRICE		📅 SAMPLED	

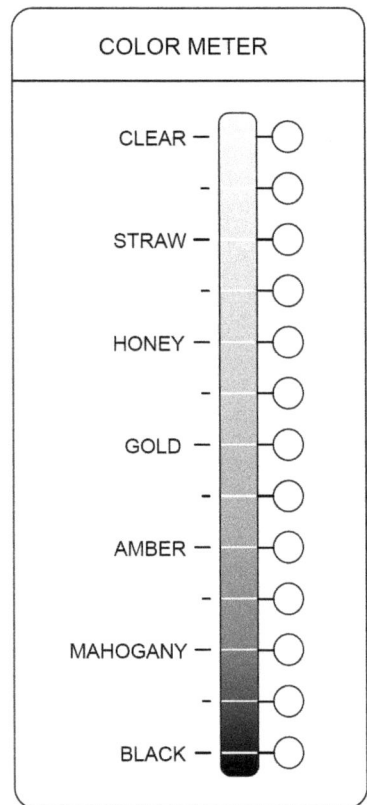

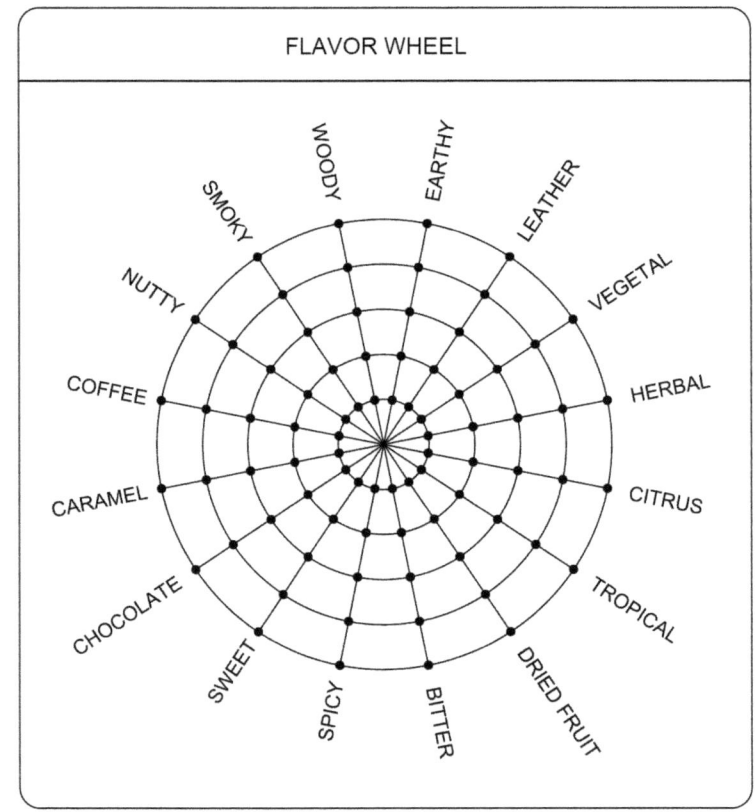

ADDITIONAL NOTES

FINAL RATING

- 🍾 APPEARANCE ☆☆☆☆☆
- 🥃 TASTE ☆☆☆☆☆
- 👄 MOUTHFEEL ☆☆☆☆☆
- ⭐ OVERALL RATING ☆☆☆☆☆

	NAME		
	DISTILLERY		TYPE
	ORIGIN		AGE
	PRICE		SAMPLED

COLOR METER

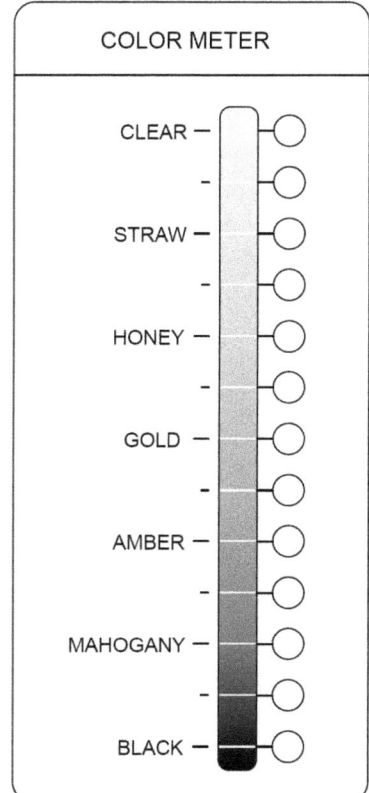

- CLEAR
- STRAW
- HONEY
- GOLD
- AMBER
- MAHOGANY
- BLACK

FLAVOR WHEEL

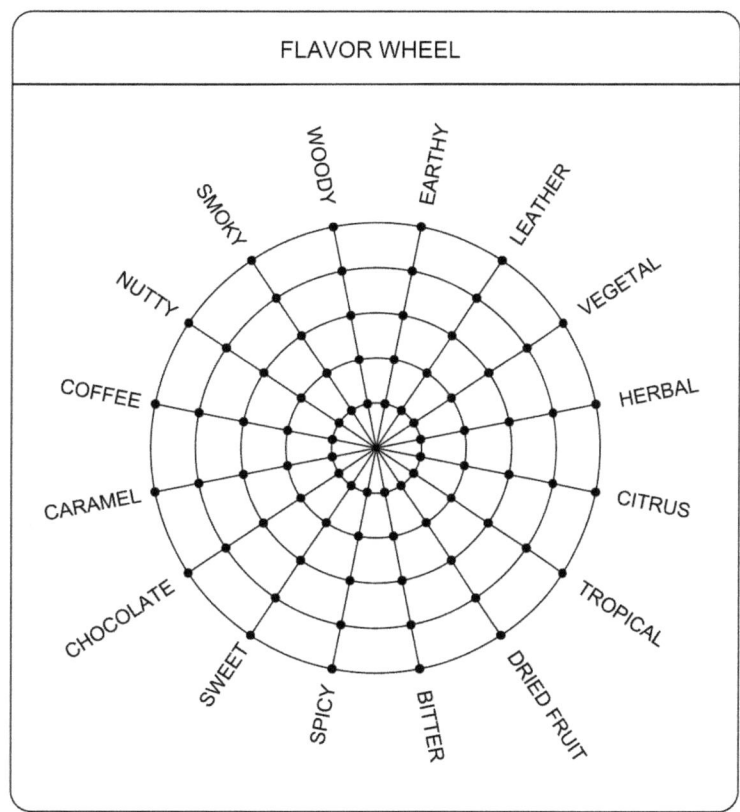

SMOKY, WOODY, EARTHY, LEATHER, VEGETAL, HERBAL, CITRUS, TROPICAL, DRIED FRUIT, BITTER, SPICY, SWEET, CHOCOLATE, CARAMEL, COFFEE, NUTTY

ADDITIONAL NOTES

FINAL RATING

- APPEARANCE ☆☆☆☆☆
- TASTE ☆☆☆☆☆
- MOUTHFEEL ☆☆☆☆☆
- OVERALL RATING ☆☆☆☆☆

	NAME		
	DISTILLERY		TYPE
	ORIGIN		AGE
	PRICE		SAMPLED

COLOR METER

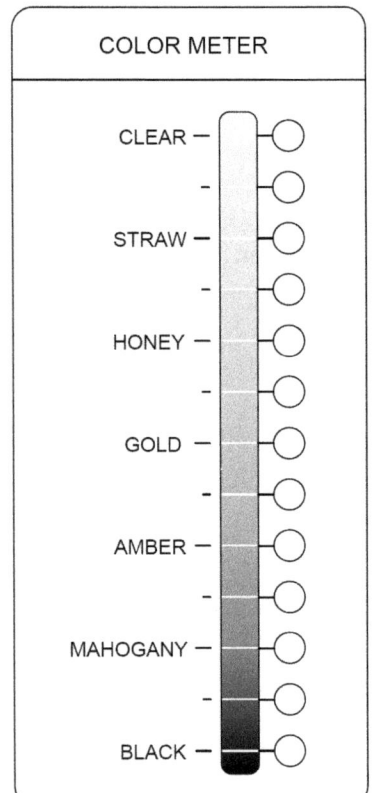

- CLEAR
- STRAW
- HONEY
- GOLD
- AMBER
- MAHOGANY
- BLACK

FLAVOR WHEEL

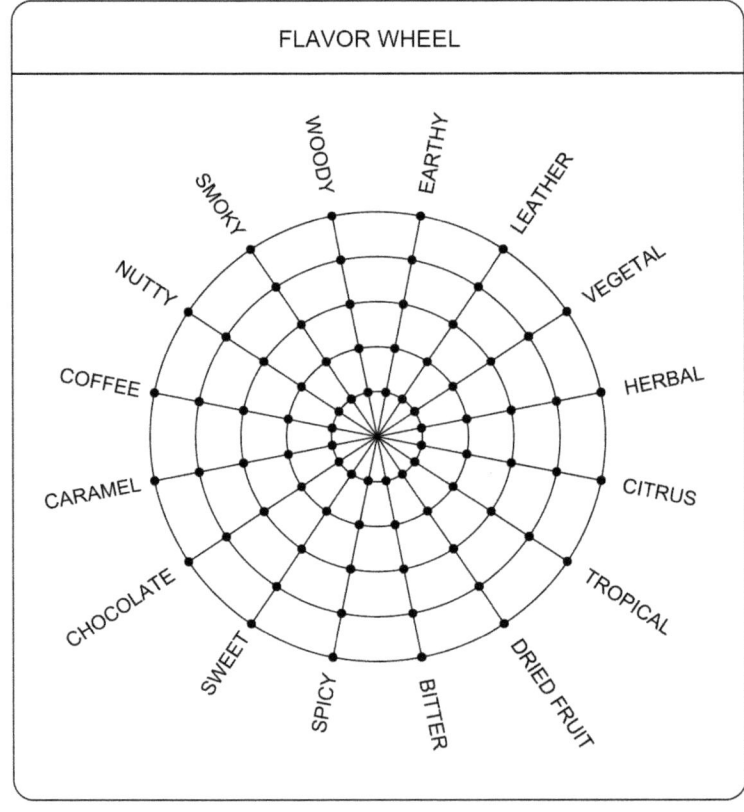

SMOKY · WOODY · EARTHY · LEATHER · VEGETAL · HERBAL · CITRUS · TROPICAL · DRIED FRUIT · BITTER · SPICY · SWEET · CHOCOLATE · CARAMEL · COFFEE · NUTTY

ADDITIONAL NOTES

FINAL RATING

- APPEARANCE ☆☆☆☆☆
- TASTE ☆☆☆☆☆
- MOUTHFEEL ☆☆☆☆☆
- OVERALL RATING ☆☆☆☆☆

NAME			
DISTILLERY		TYPE	
ORIGIN		AGE	
PRICE		SAMPLED	

COLOR METER

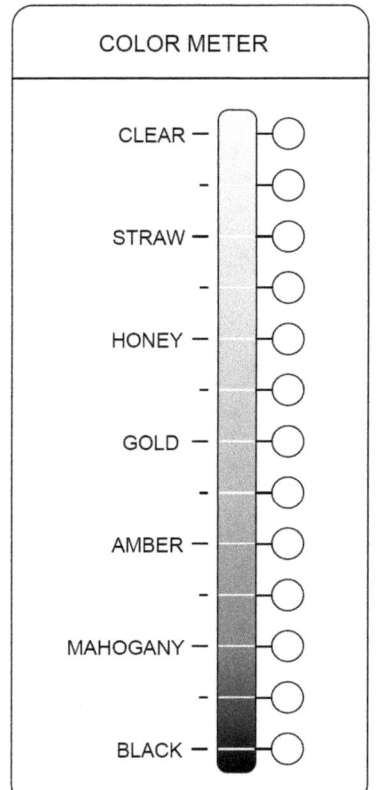

- CLEAR
- STRAW
- HONEY
- GOLD
- AMBER
- MAHOGANY
- BLACK

FLAVOR WHEEL

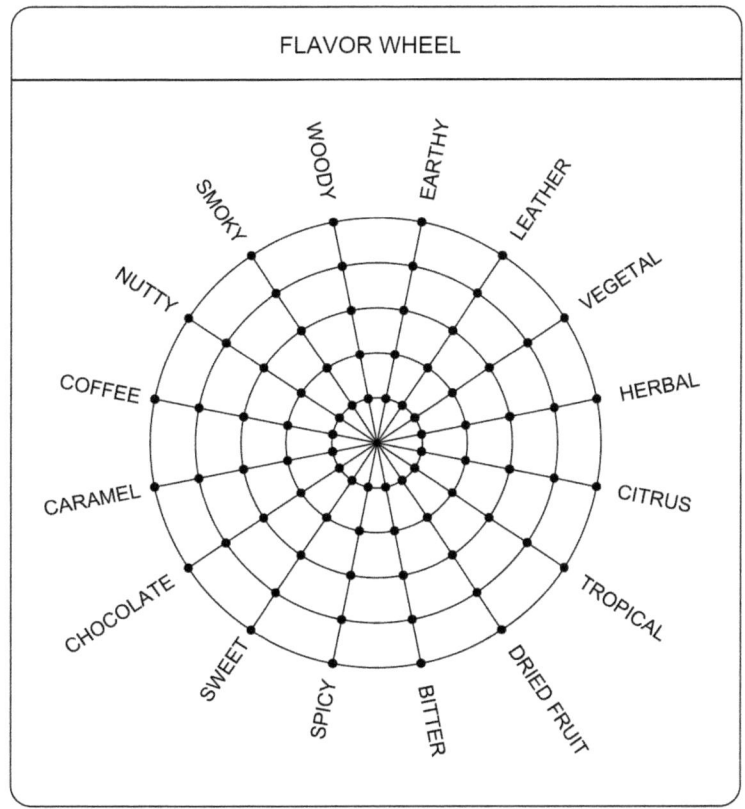

SMOKY, WOODY, EARTHY, LEATHER, VEGETAL, HERBAL, CITRUS, TROPICAL, DRIED FRUIT, BITTER, SPICY, SWEET, CHOCOLATE, CARAMEL, COFFEE, NUTTY

ADDITIONAL NOTES

FINAL RATING

- APPEARANCE ☆☆☆☆☆
- TASTE ☆☆☆☆☆
- MOUTHFEEL ☆☆☆☆☆
- OVERALL RATING ☆☆☆☆☆

	NAME		
	DISTILLERY		TYPE
	ORIGIN		AGE
	PRICE		SAMPLED

COLOR METER

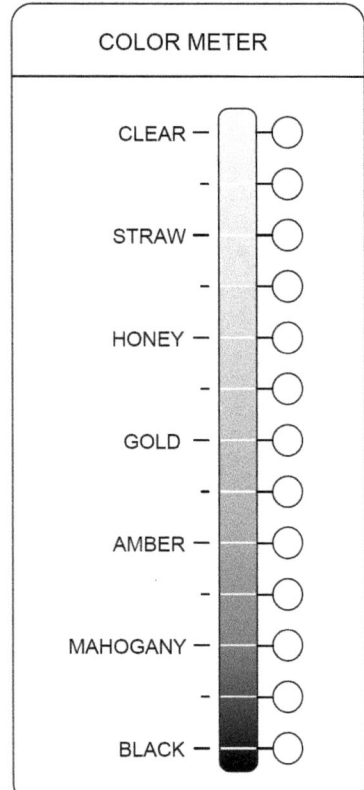

FLAVOR WHEEL

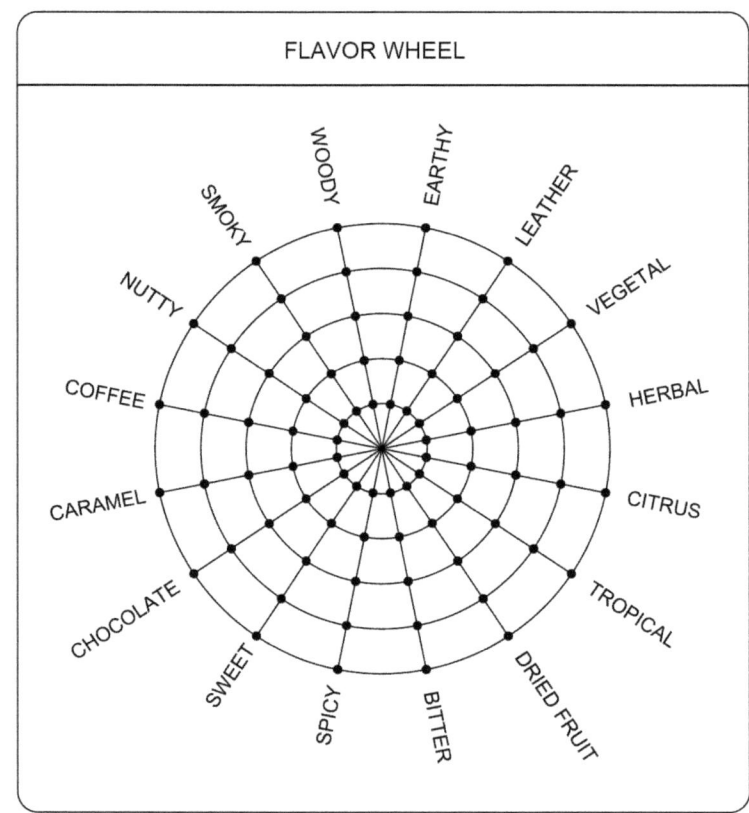

ADDITIONAL NOTES

FINAL RATING

- APPEARANCE ☆☆☆☆☆
- TASTE ☆☆☆☆☆
- MOUTHFEEL ☆☆☆☆☆
- OVERALL RATING ☆☆☆☆☆

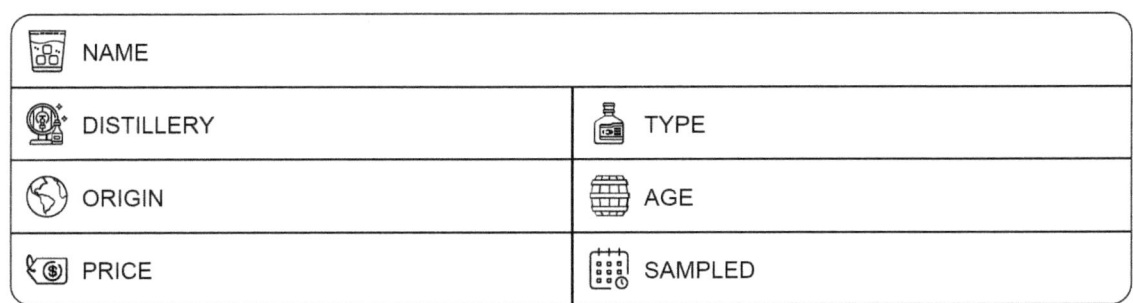

	NAME		
	DISTILLERY		TYPE
	ORIGIN		AGE
	PRICE		SAMPLED

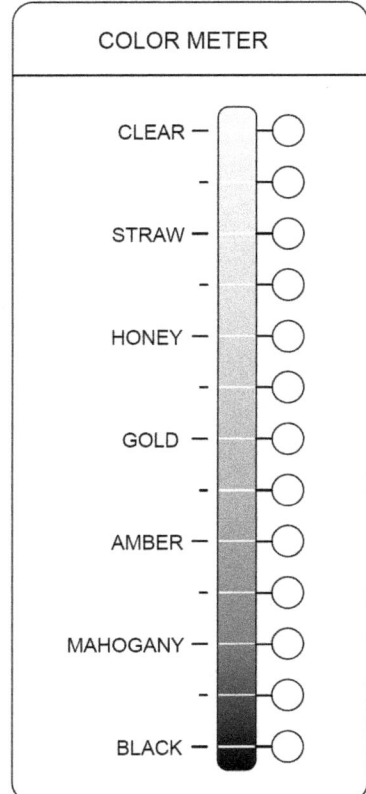

COLOR METER

- CLEAR
- STRAW
- HONEY
- GOLD
- AMBER
- MAHOGANY
- BLACK

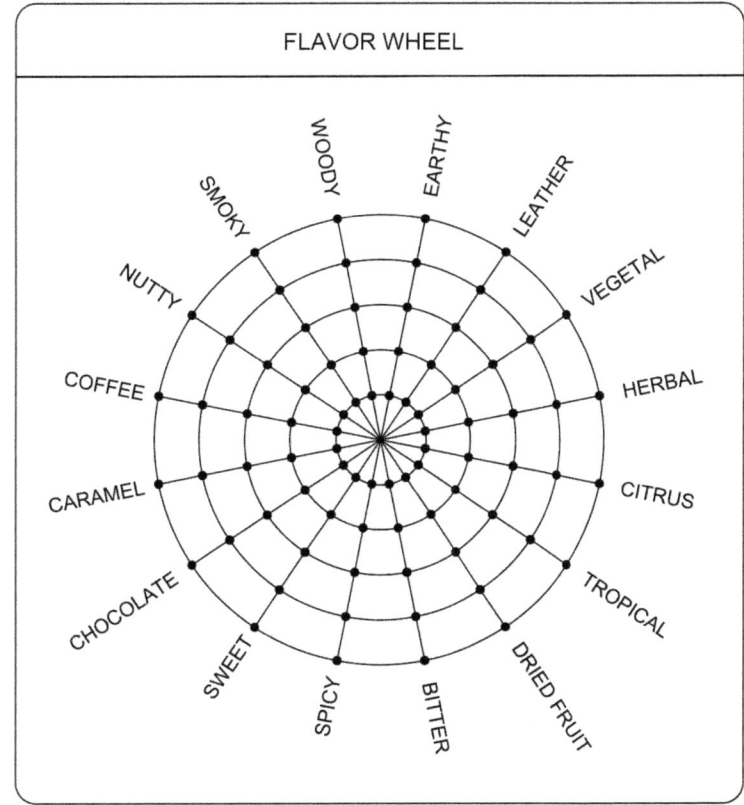

FLAVOR WHEEL

SMOKY, WOODY, EARTHY, LEATHER, VEGETAL, HERBAL, CITRUS, TROPICAL, DRIED FRUIT, BITTER, SPICY, SWEET, CHOCOLATE, CARAMEL, COFFEE, NUTTY

ADDITIONAL NOTES

FINAL RATING

- APPEARANCE ☆☆☆☆☆
- TASTE ☆☆☆☆☆
- MOUTHFEEL ☆☆☆☆☆
- OVERALL RATING ☆☆☆☆☆

	NAME		
	DISTILLERY		TYPE
	ORIGIN		AGE
	PRICE		SAMPLED

COLOR METER

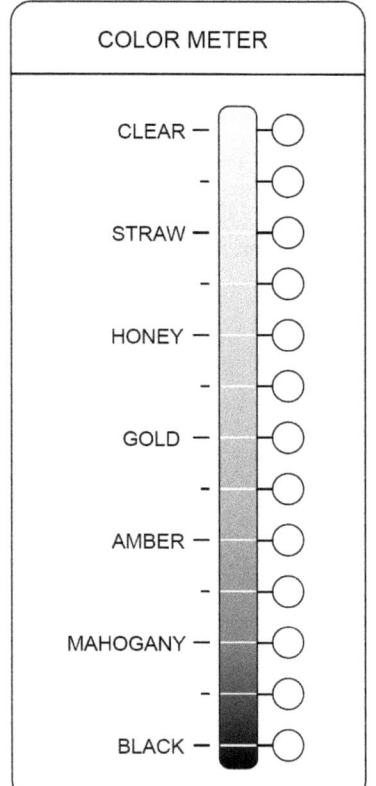

- CLEAR
- STRAW
- HONEY
- GOLD
- AMBER
- MAHOGANY
- BLACK

FLAVOR WHEEL

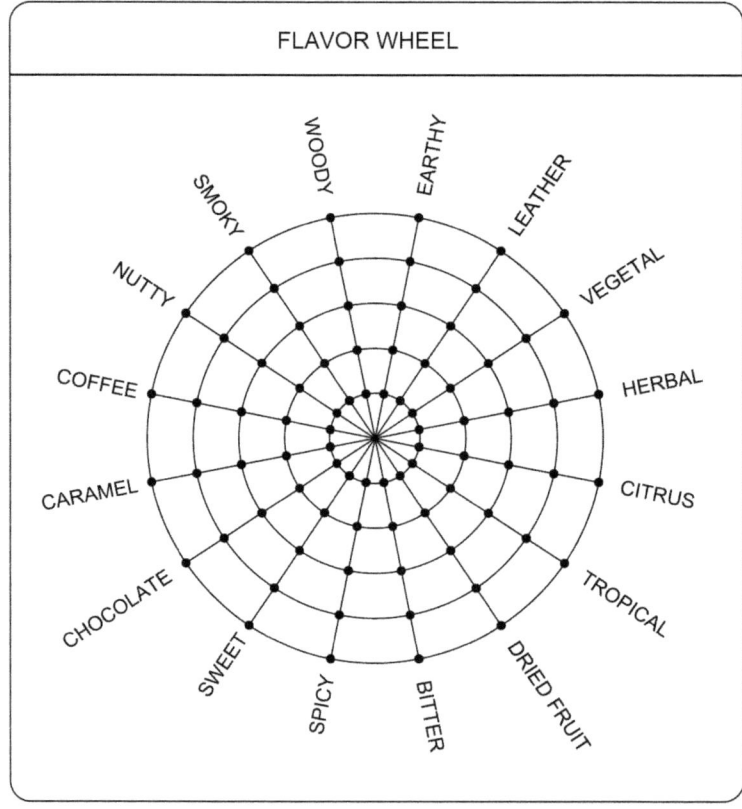

WOODY, EARTHY, LEATHER, VEGETAL, HERBAL, CITRUS, TROPICAL, DRIED FRUIT, BITTER, SPICY, SWEET, CHOCOLATE, CARAMEL, COFFEE, NUTTY, SMOKY

ADDITIONAL NOTES

FINAL RATING

- APPEARANCE ☆☆☆☆☆
- TASTE ☆☆☆☆☆
- MOUTHFEEL ☆☆☆☆☆
- OVERALL RATING ☆☆☆☆☆

	NAME		
	DISTILLERY		TYPE
	ORIGIN		AGE
	PRICE		SAMPLED

COLOR METER

- CLEAR
- STRAW
- HONEY
- GOLD
- AMBER
- MAHOGANY
- BLACK

FLAVOR WHEEL

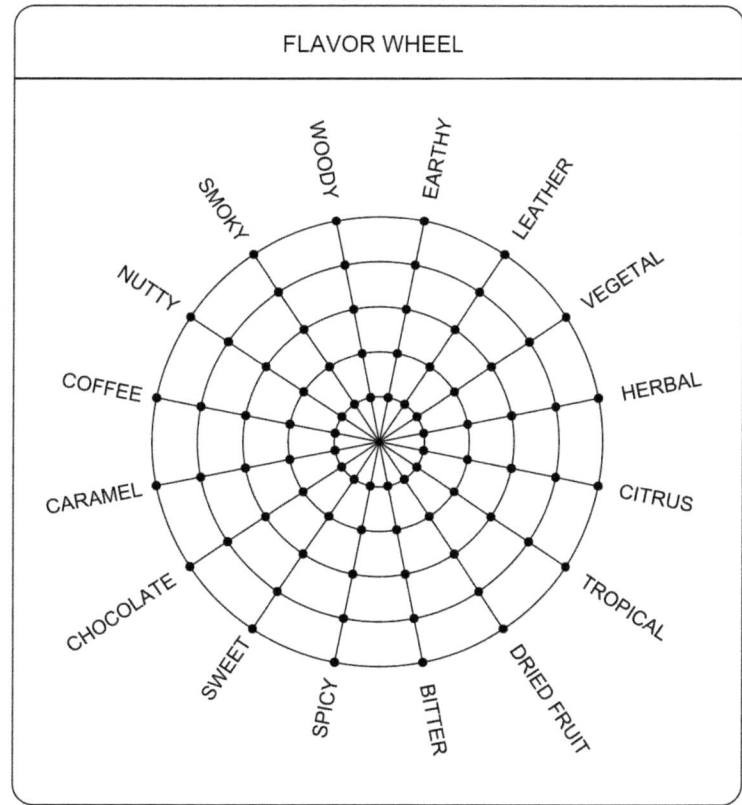

SMOKY, WOODY, EARTHY, LEATHER, VEGETAL, HERBAL, CITRUS, TROPICAL, DRIED FRUIT, BITTER, SPICY, SWEET, CHOCOLATE, CARAMEL, COFFEE, NUTTY

ADDITIONAL NOTES

FINAL RATING

- APPEARANCE ☆☆☆☆☆
- TASTE ☆☆☆☆☆
- MOUTHFEEL ☆☆☆☆☆
- OVERALL RATING ☆☆☆☆☆

NAME			
DISTILLERY		TYPE	
ORIGIN		AGE	
PRICE		SAMPLED	

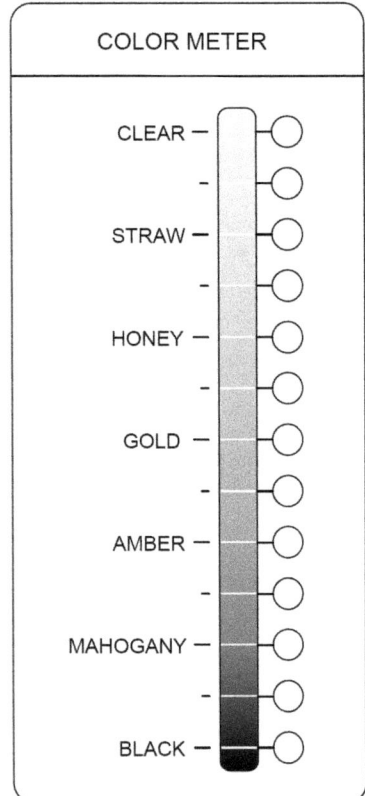

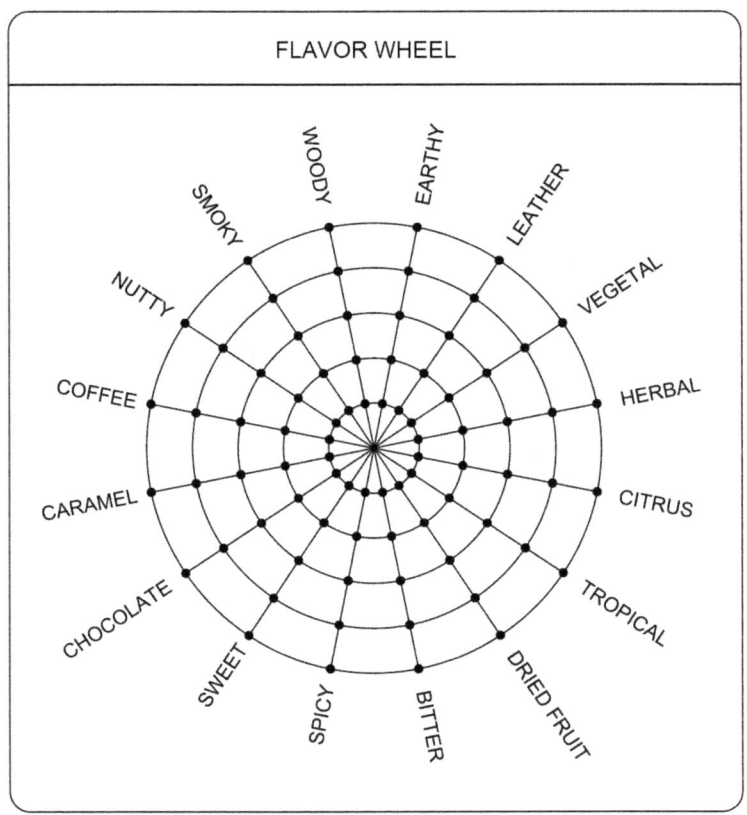

ADDITIONAL NOTES

FINAL RATING

- APPEARANCE ☆☆☆☆☆
- TASTE ☆☆☆☆☆
- MOUTHFEEL ☆☆☆☆☆
- OVERALL RATING ☆☆☆☆☆

	NAME		
	DISTILLERY		TYPE
	ORIGIN		AGE
	PRICE		SAMPLED

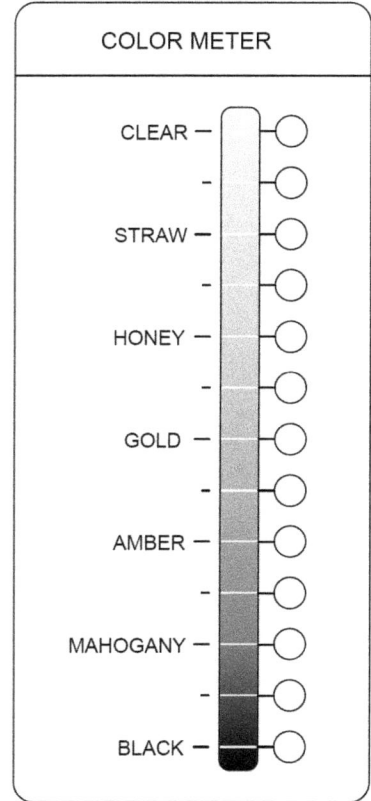

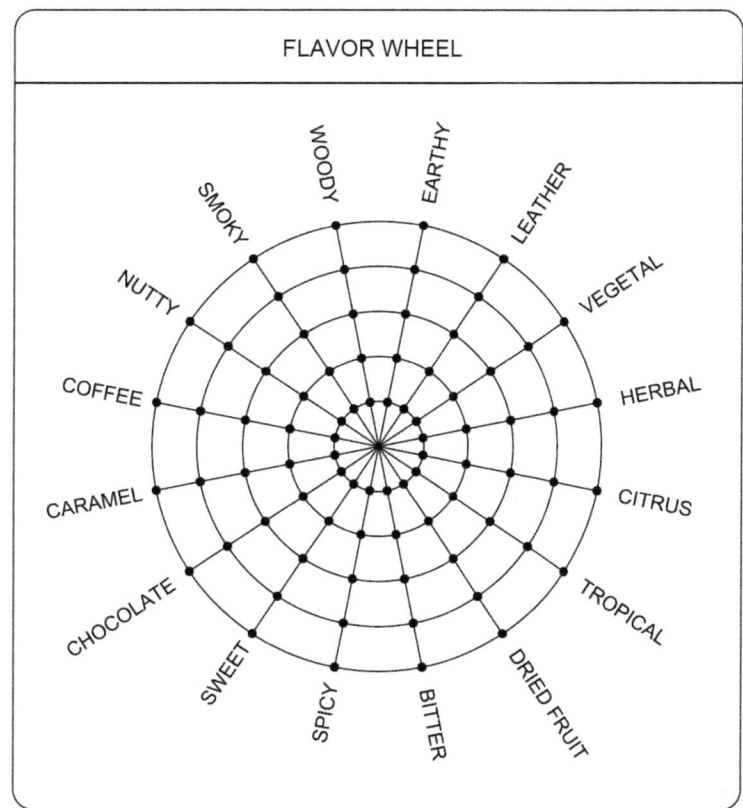

ADDITIONAL NOTES

FINAL RATING

- APPEARANCE ☆☆☆☆☆
- TASTE ☆☆☆☆☆
- MOUTHFEEL ☆☆☆☆☆
- OVERALL RATING ☆☆☆☆☆

	NAME		
	DISTILLERY		TYPE
	ORIGIN		AGE
	PRICE		SAMPLED

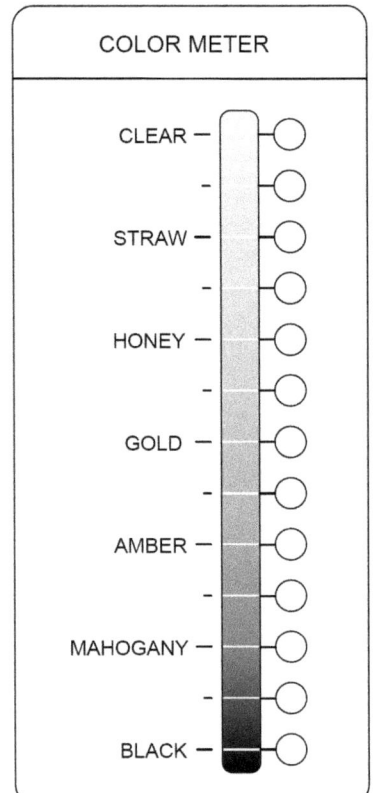

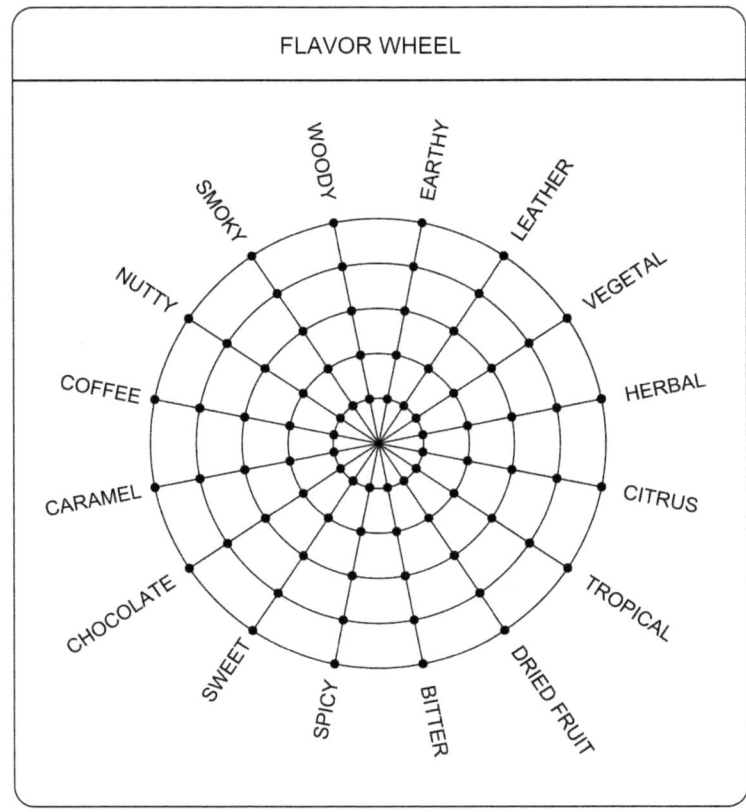

ADDITIONAL NOTES

FINAL RATING

- APPEARANCE ☆☆☆☆☆
- TASTE ☆☆☆☆☆
- MOUTHFEEL ☆☆☆☆☆
- OVERALL RATING ☆☆☆☆☆

	NAME		
	DISTILLERY		TYPE
	ORIGIN		AGE
	PRICE		SAMPLED

COLOR METER

- CLEAR
- STRAW
- HONEY
- GOLD
- AMBER
- MAHOGANY
- BLACK

FLAVOR WHEEL

SMOKY, WOODY, EARTHY, LEATHER, VEGETAL, HERBAL, CITRUS, TROPICAL, DRIED FRUIT, BITTER, SPICY, SWEET, CHOCOLATE, CARAMEL, COFFEE, NUTTY

ADDITIONAL NOTES

FINAL RATING

- APPEARANCE ☆☆☆☆☆
- TASTE ☆☆☆☆☆
- MOUTHFEEL ☆☆☆☆☆
- OVERALL RATING ☆☆☆☆☆

🥃	NAME		
🛢️	DISTILLERY	🍾 TYPE	
🌐	ORIGIN	🛢️ AGE	
💰	PRICE	📅 SAMPLED	

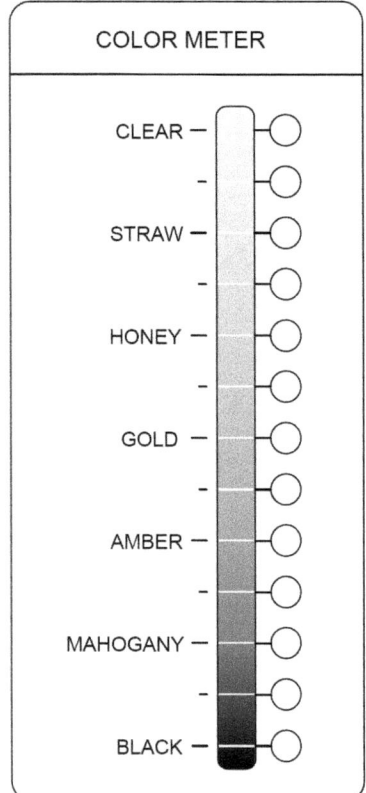

COLOR METER

- CLEAR
- STRAW
- HONEY
- GOLD
- AMBER
- MAHOGANY
- BLACK

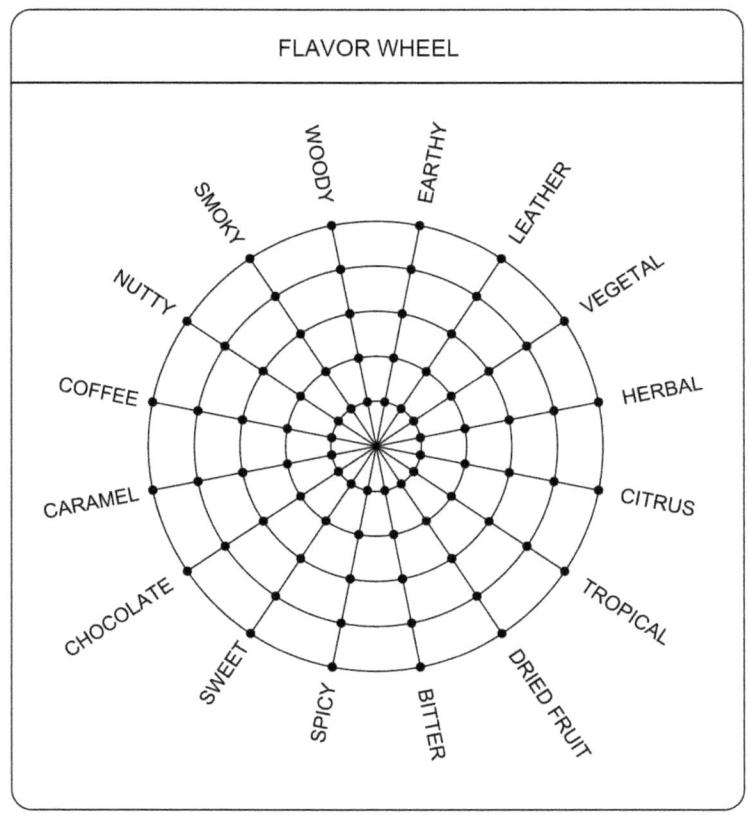

FLAVOR WHEEL

SMOKY · WOODY · EARTHY · LEATHER · VEGETAL · HERBAL · CITRUS · TROPICAL · DRIED FRUIT · BITTER · SPICY · SWEET · CHOCOLATE · CARAMEL · COFFEE · NUTTY

ADDITIONAL NOTES

FINAL RATING

- APPEARANCE ☆☆☆☆☆
- TASTE ☆☆☆☆☆
- MOUTHFEEL ☆☆☆☆☆
- OVERALL RATING ☆☆☆☆☆

NAME	

DISTILLERY		TYPE	
ORIGIN		AGE	
PRICE		SAMPLED	

COLOR METER

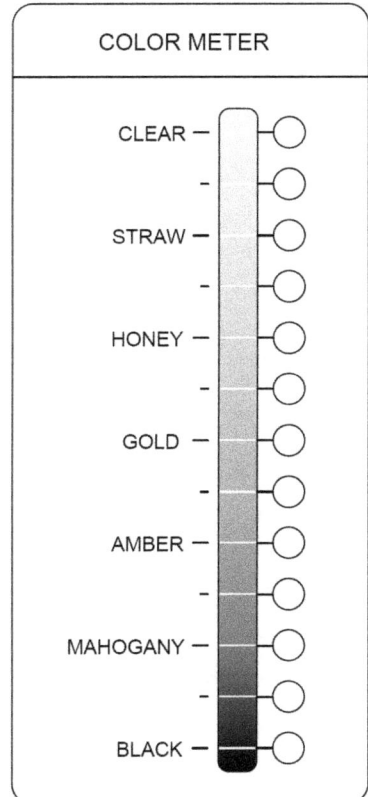

FLAVOR WHEEL

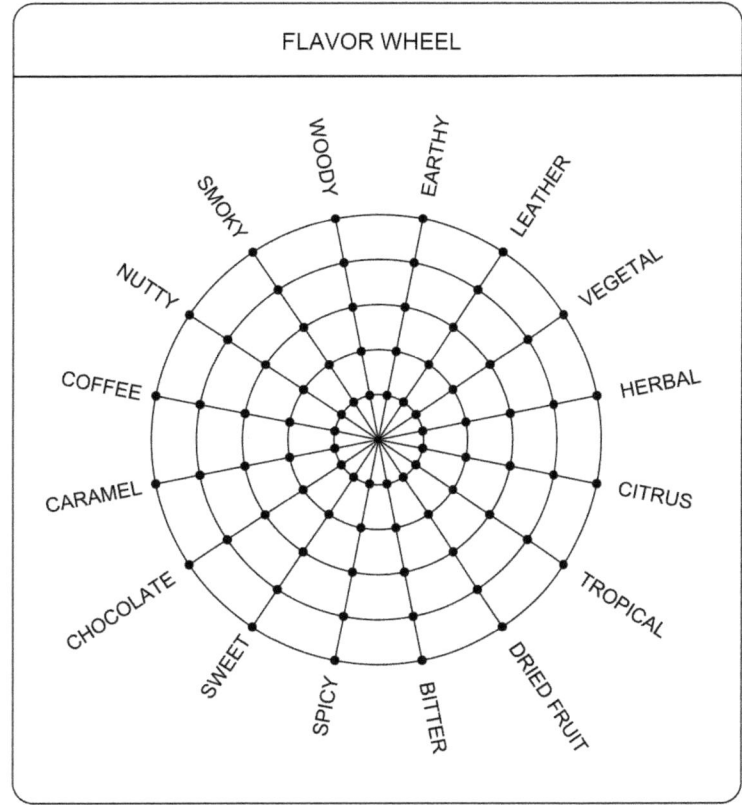

ADDITIONAL NOTES

FINAL RATING

- APPEARANCE ☆☆☆☆☆
- TASTE ☆☆☆☆☆
- MOUTHFEEL ☆☆☆☆☆
- OVERALL RATING ☆☆☆☆☆

NAME			
DISTILLERY		TYPE	
ORIGIN		AGE	
PRICE		SAMPLED	

COLOR METER

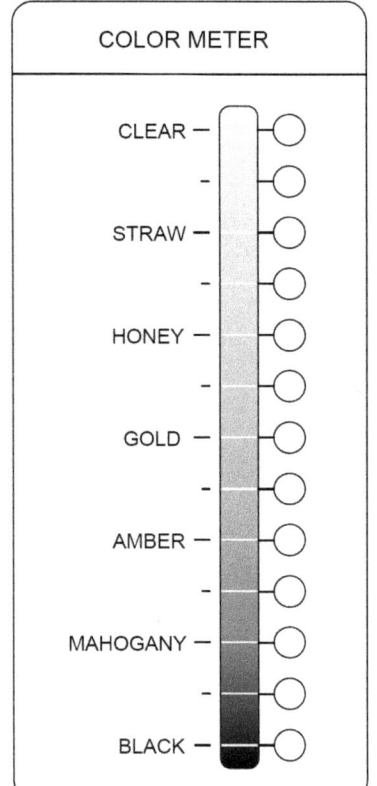

FLAVOR WHEEL

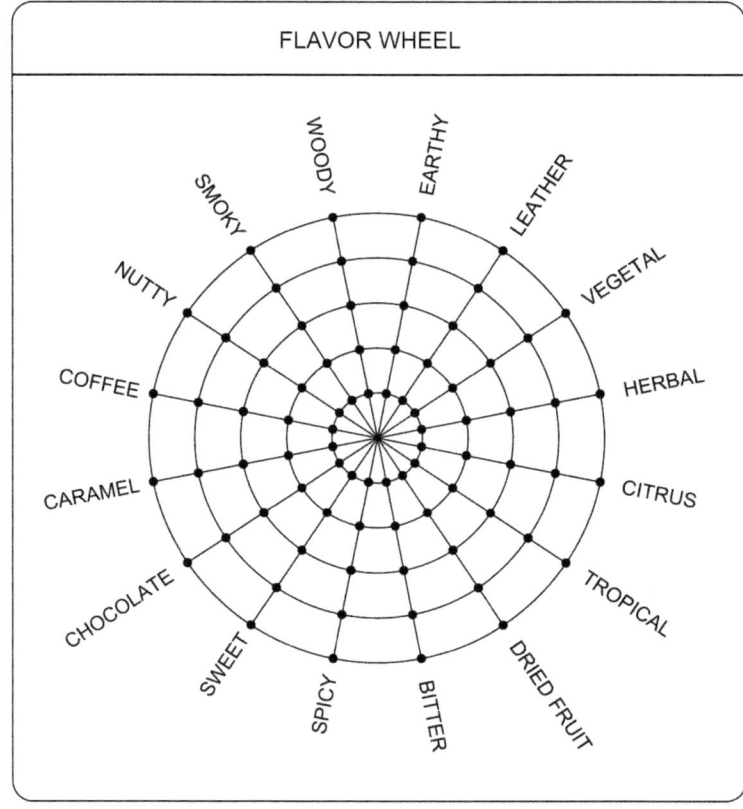

ADDITIONAL NOTES

FINAL RATING

- APPEARANCE ☆☆☆☆☆
- TASTE ☆☆☆☆☆
- MOUTHFEEL ☆☆☆☆☆
- OVERALL RATING ☆☆☆☆☆

NAME	

DISTILLERY		TYPE	
ORIGIN		AGE	
PRICE		SAMPLED	

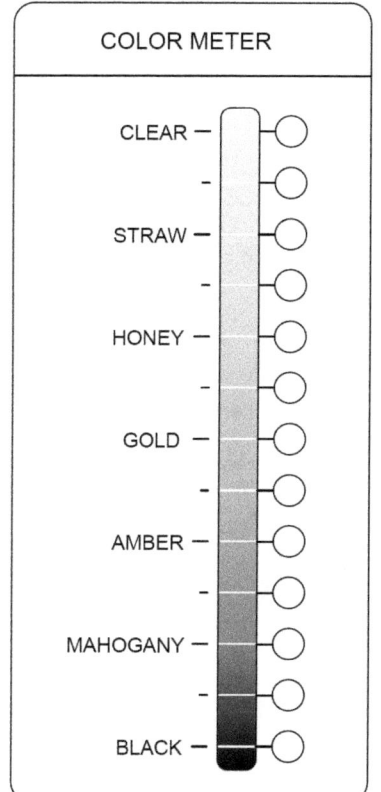

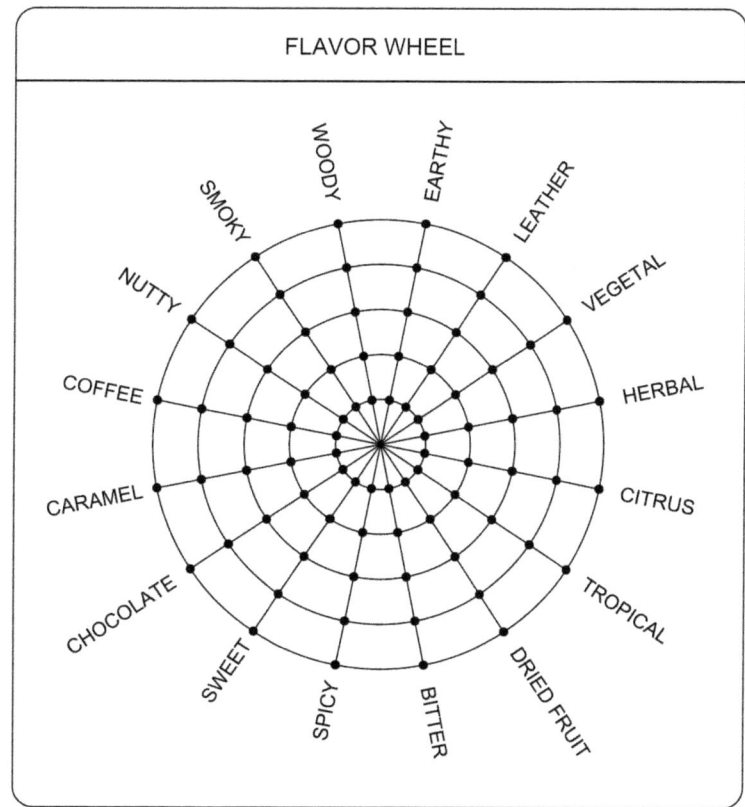

ADDITIONAL NOTES

FINAL RATING

- APPEARANCE ☆☆☆☆☆
- TASTE ☆☆☆☆☆
- MOUTHFEEL ☆☆☆☆☆
- OVERALL RATING ☆☆☆☆☆

	NAME		
	DISTILLERY		TYPE
	ORIGIN		AGE
	PRICE		SAMPLED

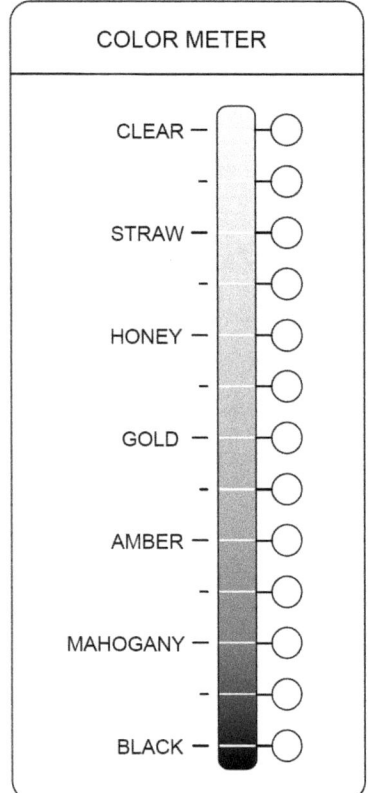

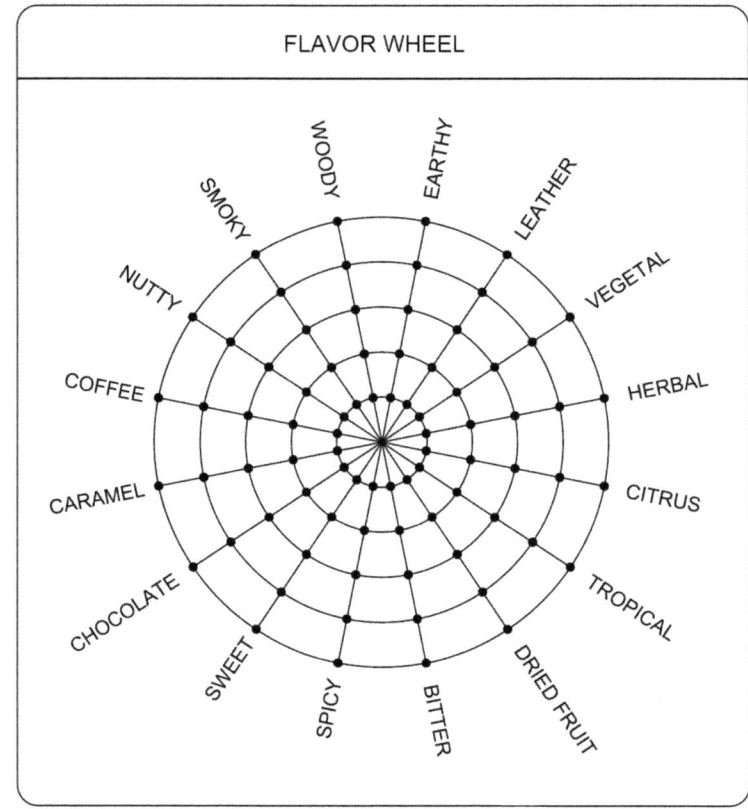

ADDITIONAL NOTES

FINAL RATING

- APPEARANCE ☆☆☆☆☆
- TASTE ☆☆☆☆☆
- MOUTHFEEL ☆☆☆☆☆
- OVERALL RATING ☆☆☆☆☆

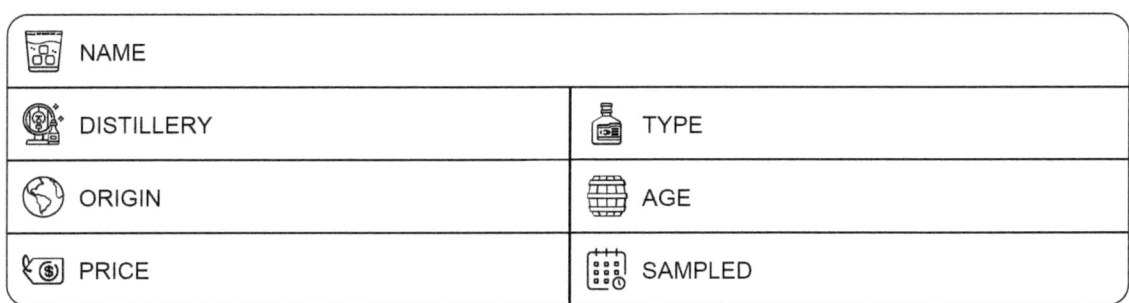

	NAME		
	DISTILLERY		TYPE
	ORIGIN		AGE
	PRICE		SAMPLED

COLOR METER

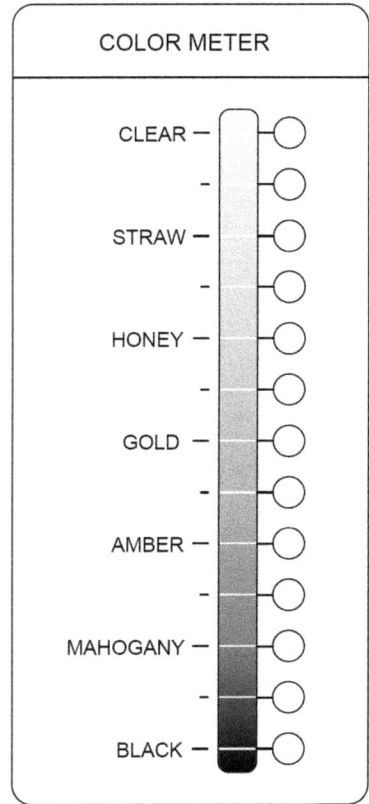

- CLEAR
- STRAW
- HONEY
- GOLD
- AMBER
- MAHOGANY
- BLACK

FLAVOR WHEEL

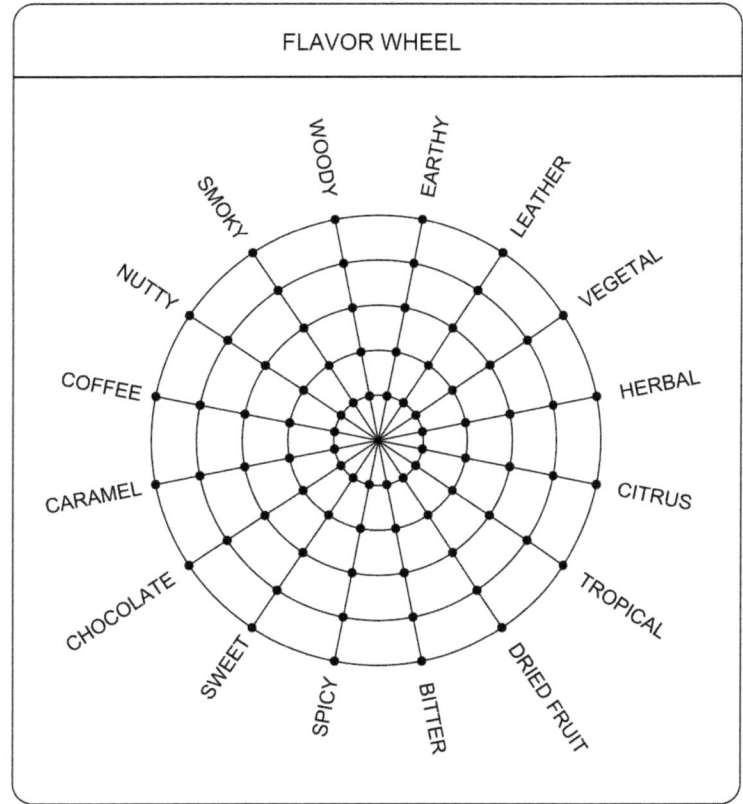

SMOKY, WOODY, EARTHY, LEATHER, NUTTY, VEGETAL, COFFEE, HERBAL, CARAMEL, CITRUS, CHOCOLATE, TROPICAL, SWEET, SPICY, BITTER, DRIED FRUIT

ADDITIONAL NOTES

FINAL RATING

- APPEARANCE ☆☆☆☆☆
- TASTE ☆☆☆☆☆
- MOUTHFEEL ☆☆☆☆☆
- OVERALL RATING ☆☆☆☆☆

	NAME		
	DISTILLERY		TYPE
	ORIGIN		AGE
	PRICE		SAMPLED

COLOR METER

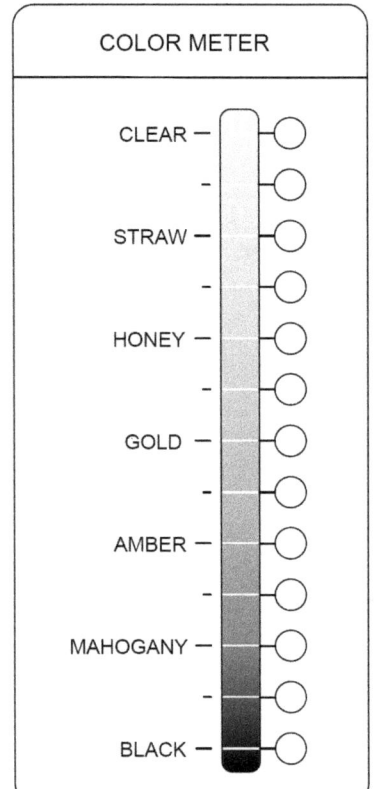

- CLEAR
- STRAW
- HONEY
- GOLD
- AMBER
- MAHOGANY
- BLACK

FLAVOR WHEEL

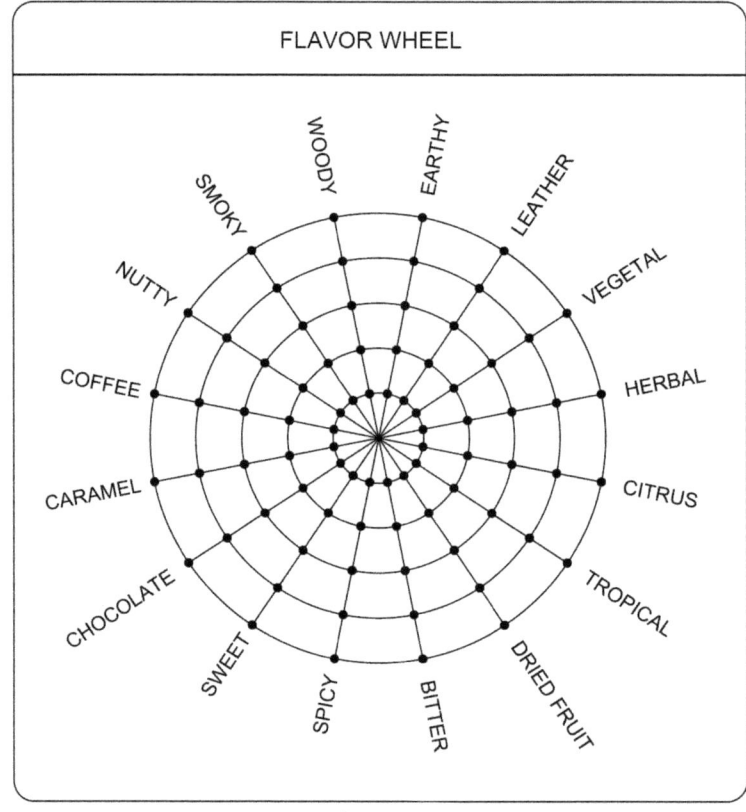

ADDITIONAL NOTES

FINAL RATING

- APPEARANCE ☆☆☆☆☆
- TASTE ☆☆☆☆☆
- MOUTHFEEL ☆☆☆☆☆
- OVERALL RATING ☆☆☆☆☆

	NAME		
	DISTILLERY		TYPE
	ORIGIN		AGE
	PRICE		SAMPLED

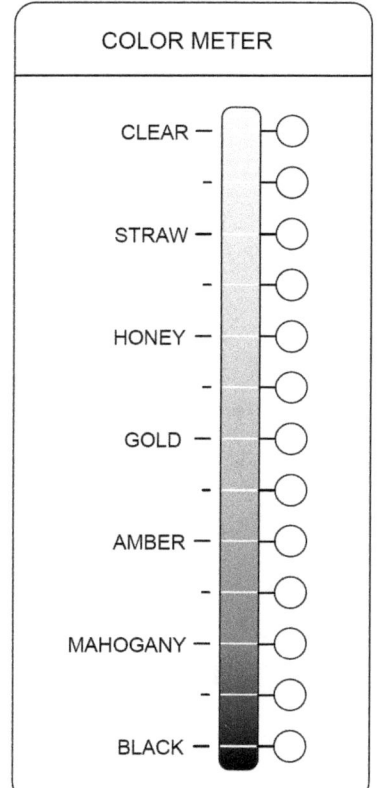

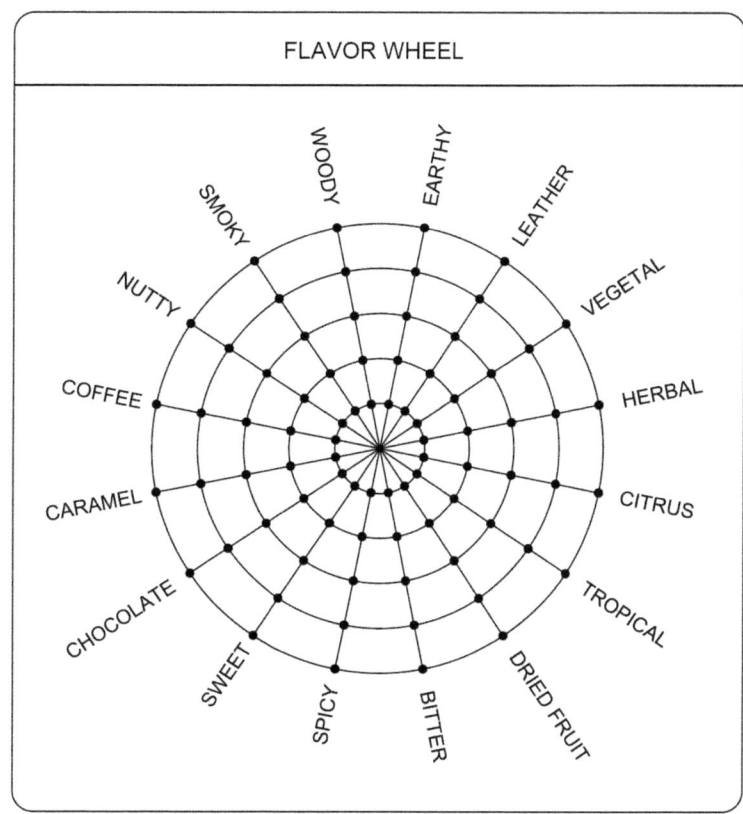

ADDITIONAL NOTES

FINAL RATING

- APPEARANCE ☆☆☆☆☆
- TASTE ☆☆☆☆☆
- MOUTHFEEL ☆☆☆☆☆
- OVERALL RATING ☆☆☆☆☆

	NAME		
	DISTILLERY		TYPE
	ORIGIN		AGE
	PRICE		SAMPLED

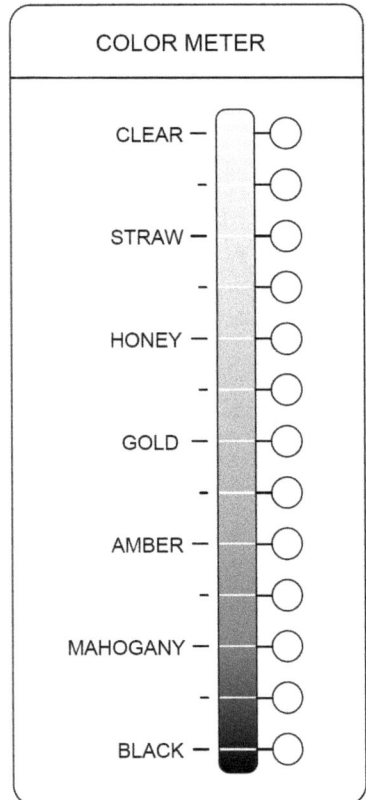

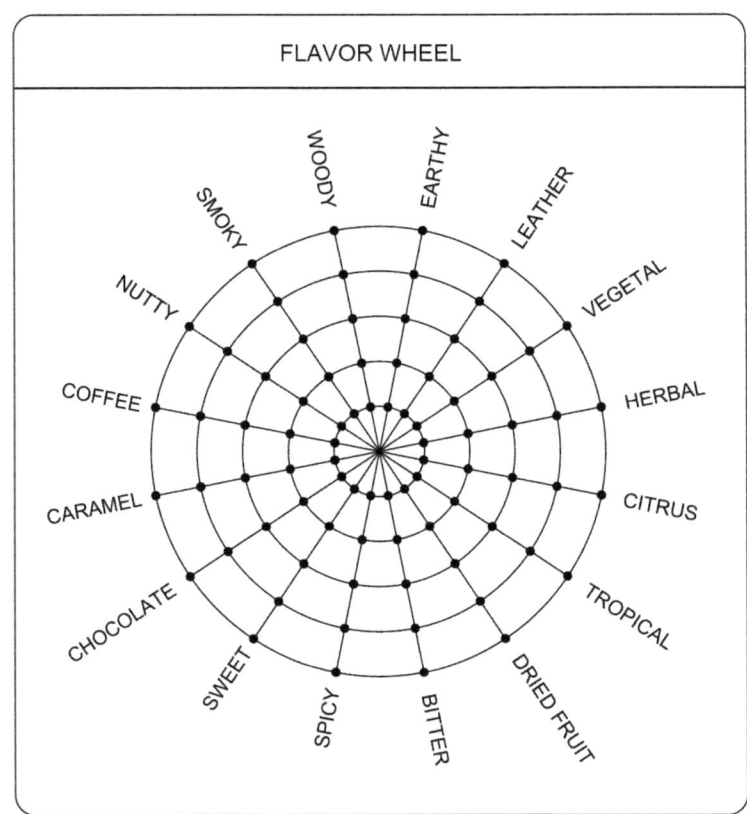

ADDITIONAL NOTES

FINAL RATING

- APPEARANCE ☆☆☆☆☆
- TASTE ☆☆☆☆☆
- MOUTHFEEL ☆☆☆☆☆
- OVERALL RATING ☆☆☆☆☆

	NAME		
	DISTILLERY		TYPE
	ORIGIN		AGE
	PRICE		SAMPLED

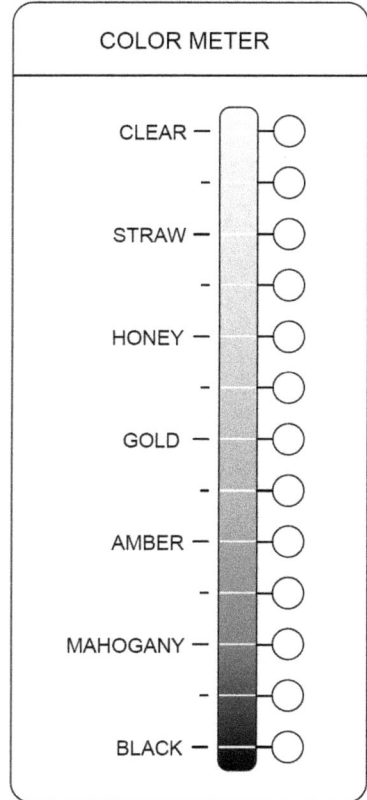

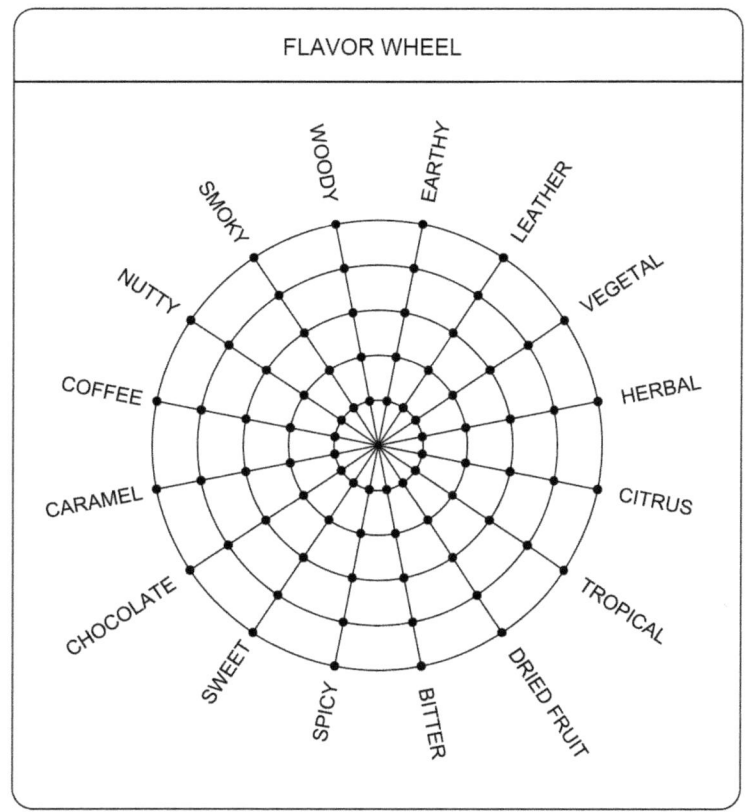

ADDITIONAL NOTES

FINAL RATING

- APPEARANCE ☆☆☆☆☆
- TASTE ☆☆☆☆☆
- MOUTHFEEL ☆☆☆☆☆
- OVERALL RATING ☆☆☆☆☆

NAME			
DISTILLERY		TYPE	
ORIGIN		AGE	
PRICE		SAMPLED	

COLOR METER

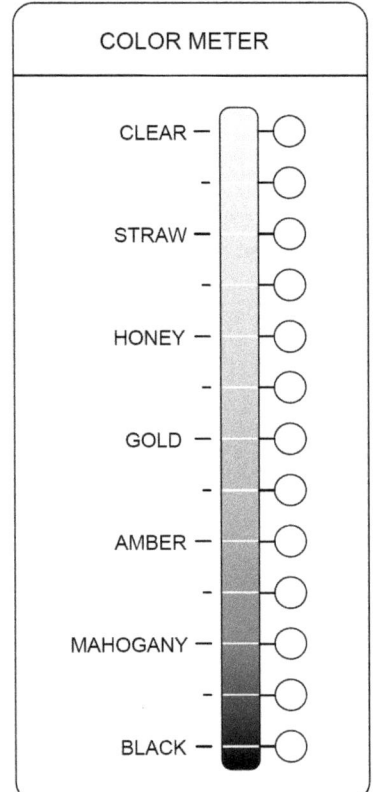

- CLEAR
- STRAW
- HONEY
- GOLD
- AMBER
- MAHOGANY
- BLACK

FLAVOR WHEEL

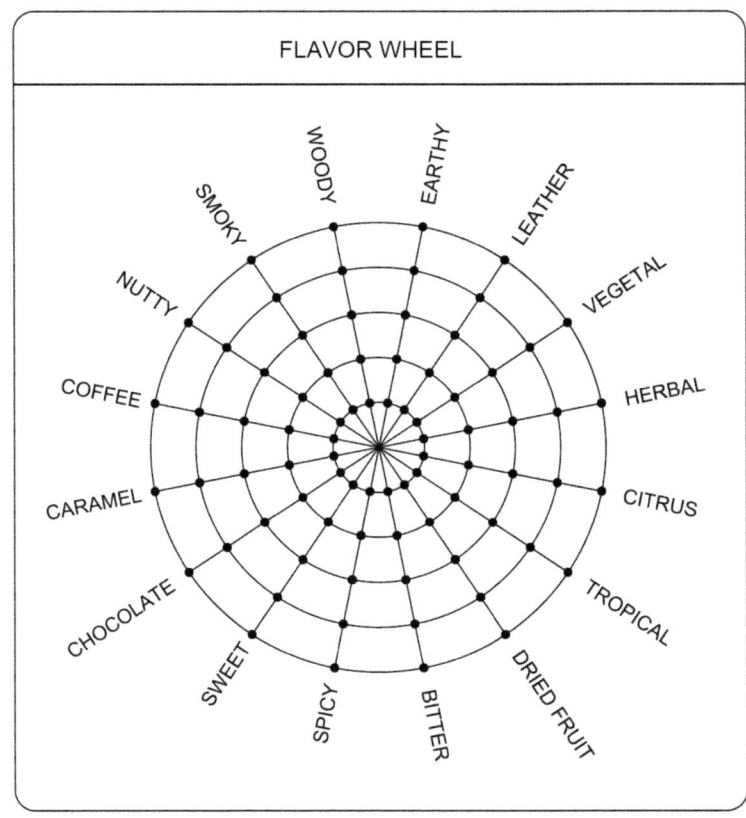

SMOKY, WOODY, EARTHY, LEATHER, VEGETAL, HERBAL, CITRUS, TROPICAL, DRIED FRUIT, BITTER, SPICY, SWEET, CHOCOLATE, CARAMEL, COFFEE, NUTTY

ADDITIONAL NOTES

FINAL RATING

- APPEARANCE ☆☆☆☆☆
- TASTE ☆☆☆☆☆
- MOUTHFEEL ☆☆☆☆☆
- OVERALL RATING ☆☆☆☆☆

	NAME		
	DISTILLERY		TYPE
	ORIGIN		AGE
	PRICE		SAMPLED

COLOR METER

- CLEAR
- STRAW
- HONEY
- GOLD
- AMBER
- MAHOGANY
- BLACK

FLAVOR WHEEL

SMOKY · WOODY · EARTHY · LEATHER · VEGETAL · HERBAL · CITRUS · TROPICAL · DRIED FRUIT · BITTER · SPICY · SWEET · CHOCOLATE · CARAMEL · COFFEE · NUTTY

ADDITIONAL NOTES

FINAL RATING

- APPEARANCE ☆☆☆☆☆
- TASTE ☆☆☆☆☆
- MOUTHFEEL ☆☆☆☆☆
- OVERALL RATING ☆☆☆☆☆

NAME	
DISTILLERY	TYPE
ORIGIN	AGE
PRICE	SAMPLED

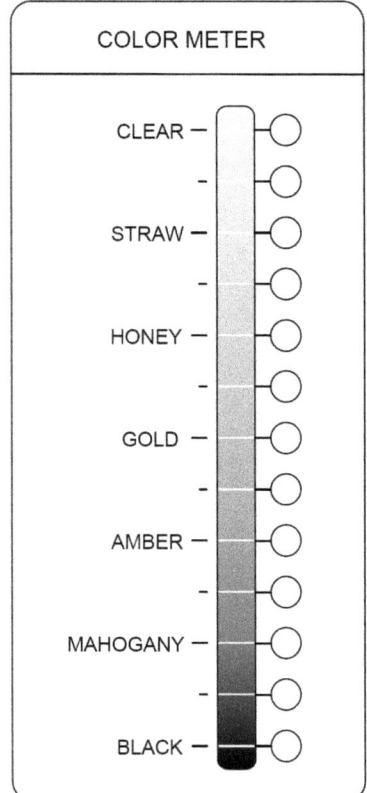

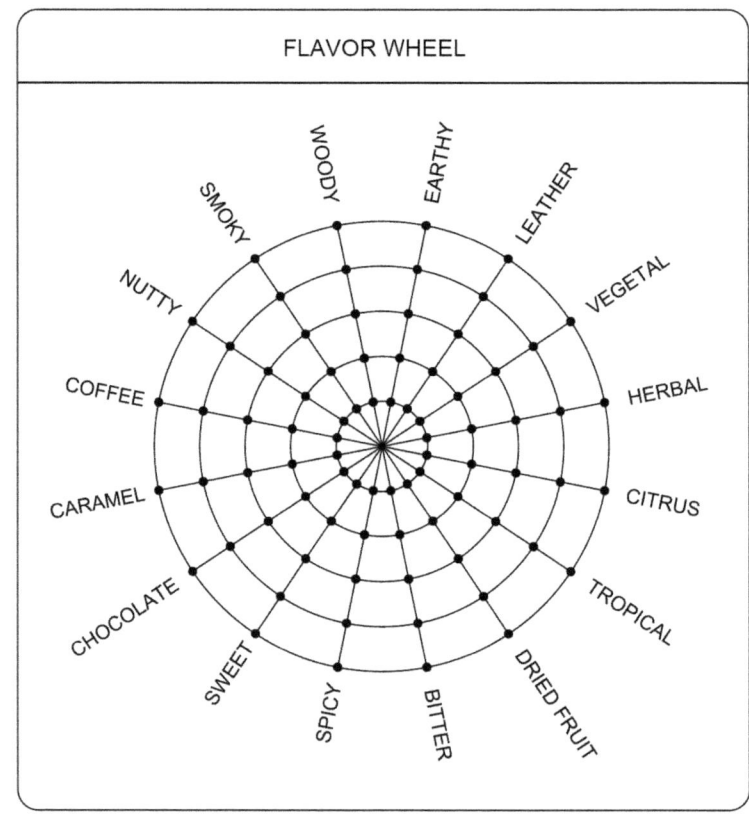

ADDITIONAL NOTES

FINAL RATING

- APPEARANCE ☆☆☆☆☆
- TASTE ☆☆☆☆☆
- MOUTHFEEL ☆☆☆☆☆
- OVERALL RATING ☆☆☆☆☆

	NAME		
	DISTILLERY		TYPE
	ORIGIN		AGE
	PRICE		SAMPLED

COLOR METER

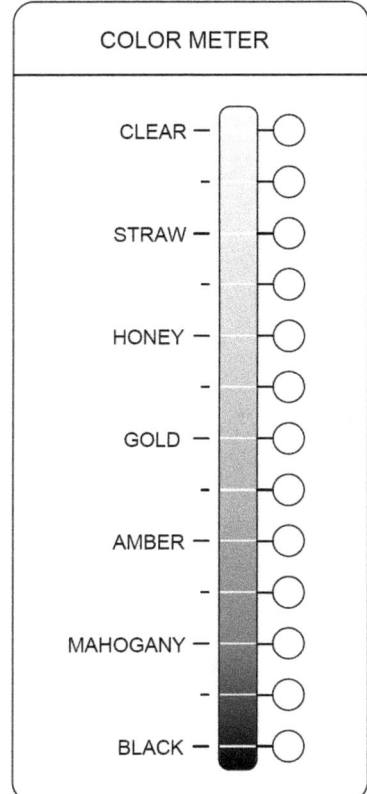

FLAVOR WHEEL

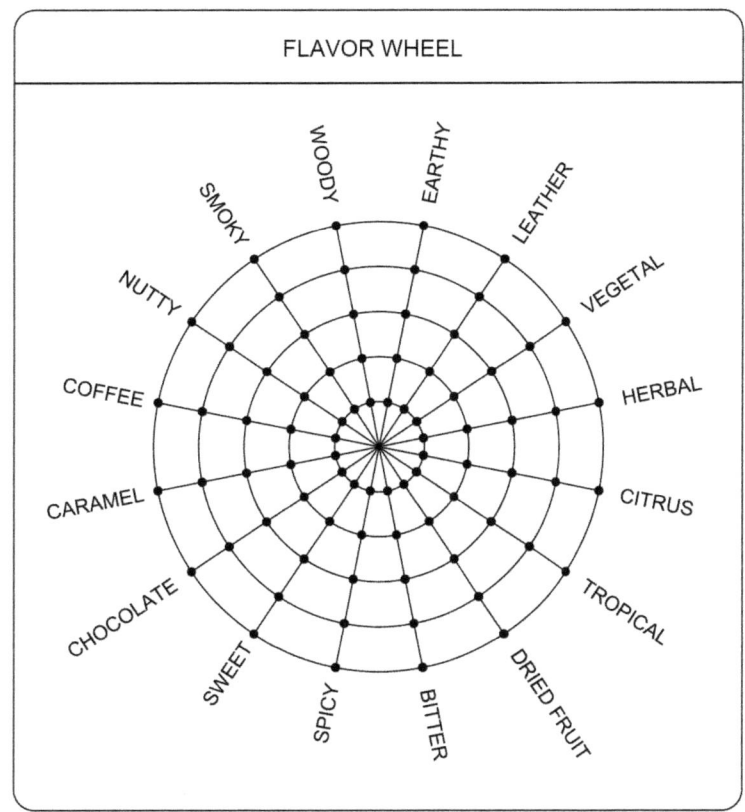

ADDITIONAL NOTES

FINAL RATING

- APPEARANCE ☆☆☆☆☆
- TASTE ☆☆☆☆☆
- MOUTHFEEL ☆☆☆☆☆
- OVERALL RATING ☆☆☆☆☆

	NAME		
	DISTILLERY		TYPE
	ORIGIN		AGE
	PRICE		SAMPLED

COLOR METER

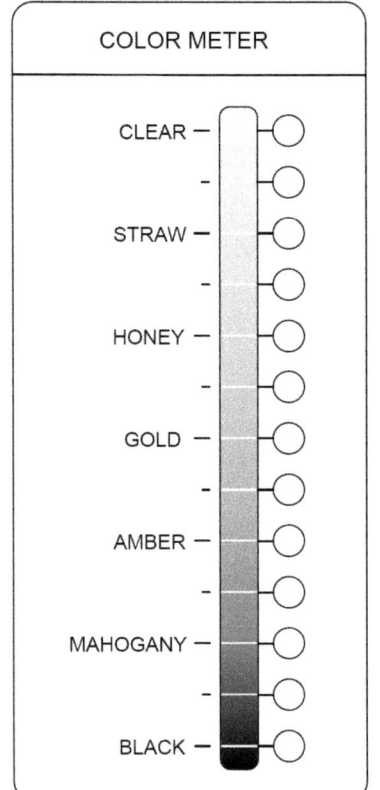

- CLEAR
- STRAW
- HONEY
- GOLD
- AMBER
- MAHOGANY
- BLACK

FLAVOR WHEEL

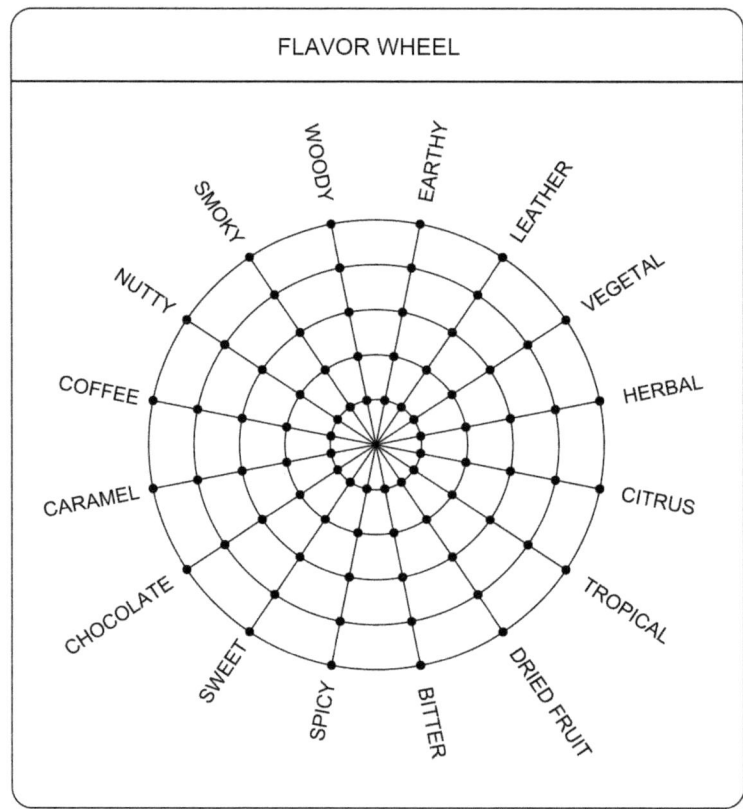

SMOKY, WOODY, EARTHY, LEATHER, NUTTY, VEGETAL, COFFEE, HERBAL, CARAMEL, CITRUS, CHOCOLATE, TROPICAL, SWEET, SPICY, BITTER, DRIED FRUIT

ADDITIONAL NOTES

FINAL RATING

- APPEARANCE ☆☆☆☆☆
- TASTE ☆☆☆☆☆
- MOUTHFEEL ☆☆☆☆☆
- OVERALL RATING ☆☆☆☆☆

	NAME		
	DISTILLERY		TYPE
	ORIGIN		AGE
	PRICE		SAMPLED

COLOR METER

- CLEAR
- STRAW
- HONEY
- GOLD
- AMBER
- MAHOGANY
- BLACK

FLAVOR WHEEL

SMOKY, WOODY, EARTHY, LEATHER, VEGETAL, NUTTY, HERBAL, COFFEE, CITRUS, CARAMEL, TROPICAL, CHOCOLATE, DRIED FRUIT, SWEET, SPICY, BITTER

ADDITIONAL NOTES

FINAL RATING

- APPEARANCE ☆☆☆☆☆
- TASTE ☆☆☆☆☆
- MOUTHFEEL ☆☆☆☆☆
- OVERALL RATING ☆☆☆☆☆

NAME			
DISTILLERY		TYPE	
ORIGIN		AGE	
PRICE		SAMPLED	

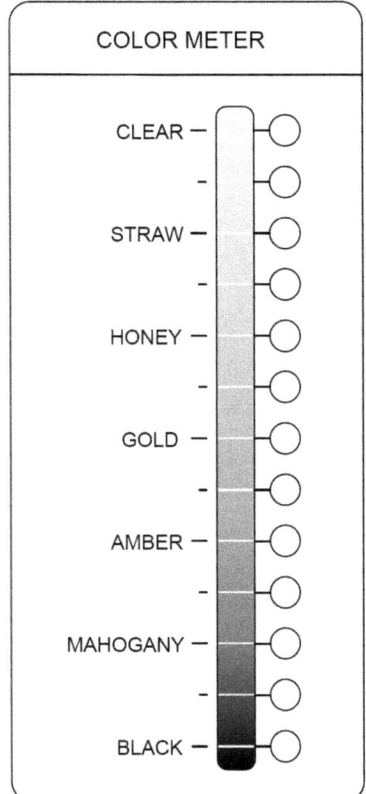

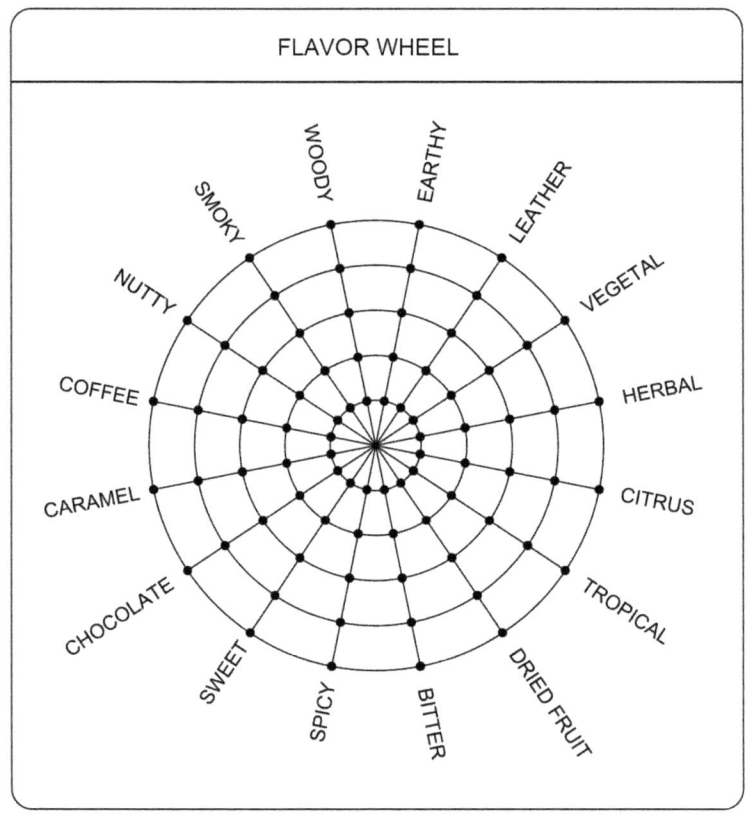

ADDITIONAL NOTES

FINAL RATING

- APPEARANCE ☆☆☆☆☆
- TASTE ☆☆☆☆☆
- MOUTHFEEL ☆☆☆☆☆
- OVERALL RATING ☆☆☆☆☆

	NAME		
	DISTILLERY		TYPE
	ORIGIN		AGE
	PRICE		SAMPLED

COLOR METER

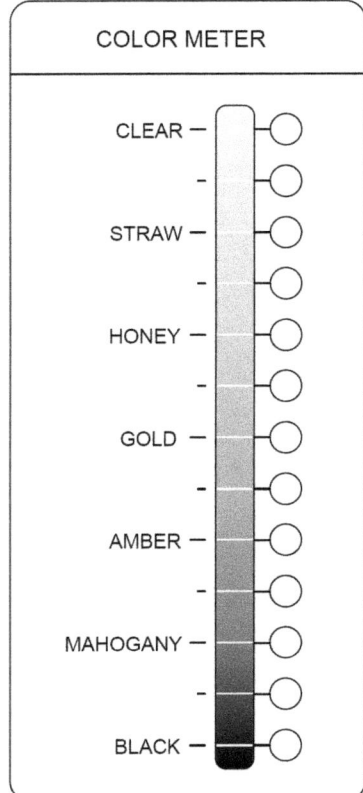

- CLEAR
- STRAW
- HONEY
- GOLD
- AMBER
- MAHOGANY
- BLACK

FLAVOR WHEEL

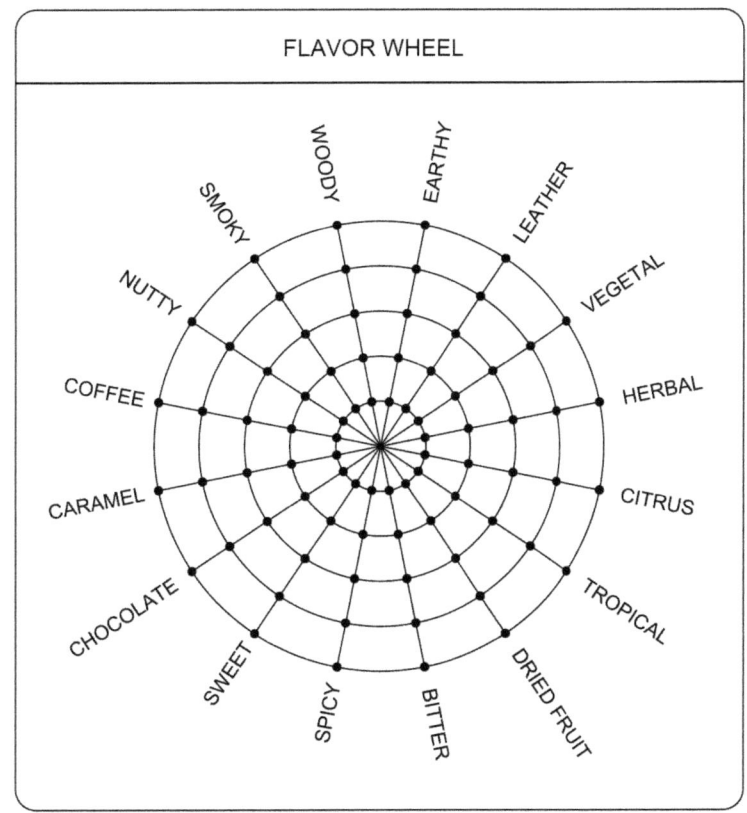

SMOKY, WOODY, EARTHY, LEATHER, NUTTY, VEGETAL, COFFEE, HERBAL, CARAMEL, CITRUS, CHOCOLATE, TROPICAL, SWEET, SPICY, BITTER, DRIED FRUIT

ADDITIONAL NOTES

FINAL RATING

- APPEARANCE ☆☆☆☆☆
- TASTE ☆☆☆☆☆
- MOUTHFEEL ☆☆☆☆☆
- OVERALL RATING ☆☆☆☆☆

🥃 NAME			
🛢️ DISTILLERY		🍾 TYPE	
🌍 ORIGIN		🛢️ AGE	
💰 PRICE		📅 SAMPLED	

COLOR METER

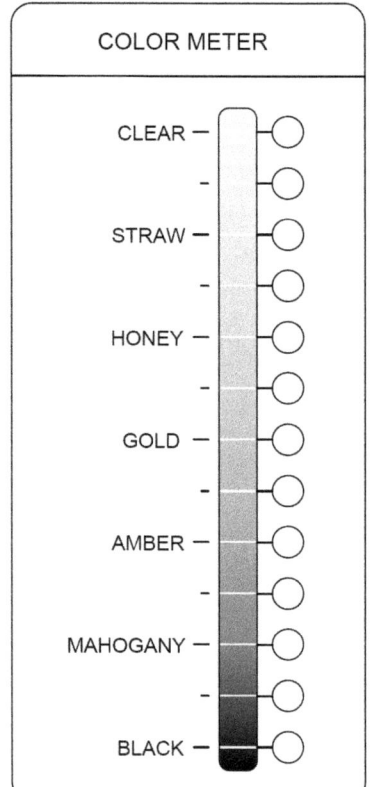

- CLEAR
- STRAW
- HONEY
- GOLD
- AMBER
- MAHOGANY
- BLACK

FLAVOR WHEEL

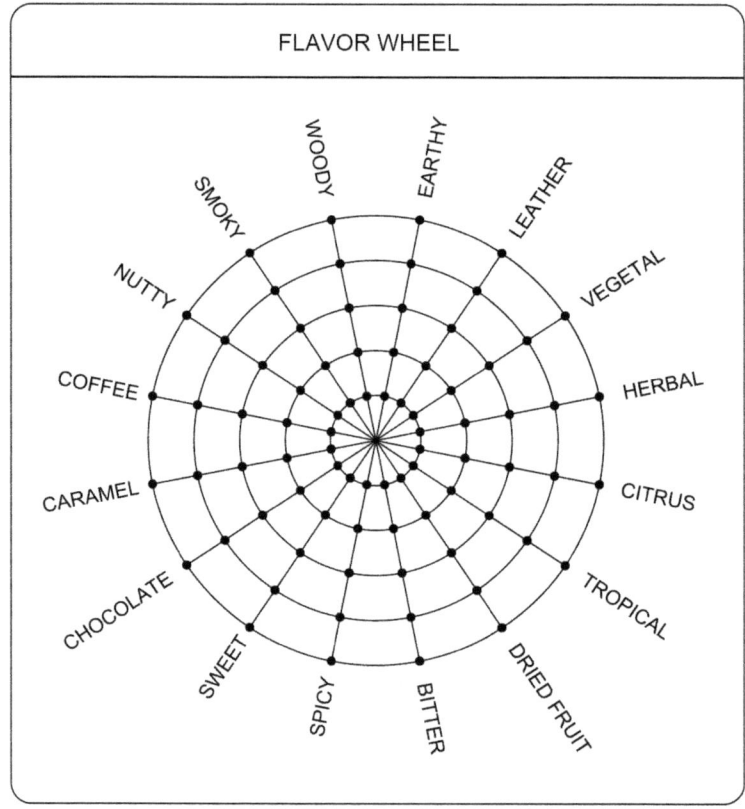

WOODY, EARTHY, LEATHER, VEGETAL, HERBAL, CITRUS, TROPICAL, DRIED FRUIT, BITTER, SPICY, SWEET, CHOCOLATE, CARAMEL, COFFEE, NUTTY, SMOKY

ADDITIONAL NOTES

FINAL RATING

- APPEARANCE ☆☆☆☆☆
- TASTE ☆☆☆☆☆
- MOUTHFEEL ☆☆☆☆☆
- OVERALL RATING ☆☆☆☆☆

🥃 NAME	
🛢️ DISTILLERY	🍾 TYPE
🌍 ORIGIN	🛢️ AGE
💰 PRICE	📅 SAMPLED

COLOR METER

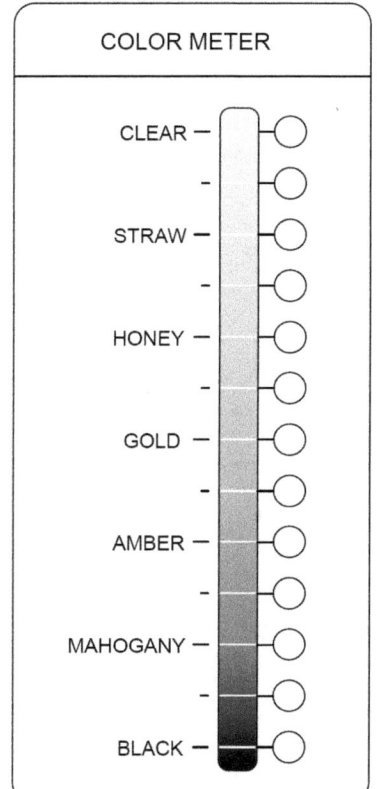

- CLEAR
- STRAW
- HONEY
- GOLD
- AMBER
- MAHOGANY
- BLACK

FLAVOR WHEEL

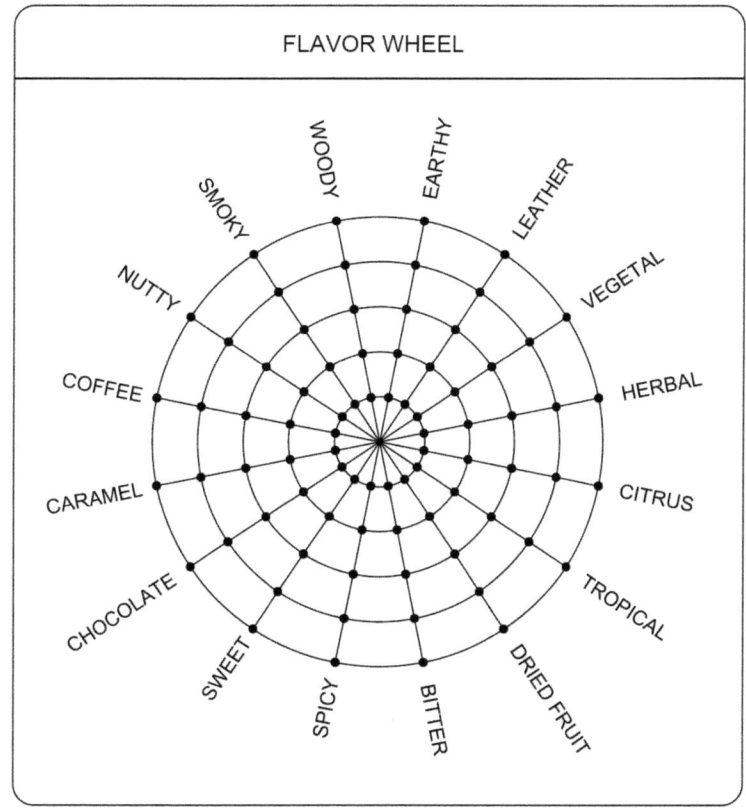

SMOKY, WOODY, EARTHY, LEATHER, NUTTY, VEGETAL, COFFEE, HERBAL, CARAMEL, CITRUS, CHOCOLATE, TROPICAL, SWEET, SPICY, BITTER, DRIED FRUIT

ADDITIONAL NOTES

FINAL RATING

- APPEARANCE ☆☆☆☆☆
- TASTE ☆☆☆☆☆
- MOUTHFEEL ☆☆☆☆☆
- OVERALL RATING ☆☆☆☆☆

	NAME		
	DISTILLERY		TYPE
	ORIGIN		AGE
	PRICE		SAMPLED

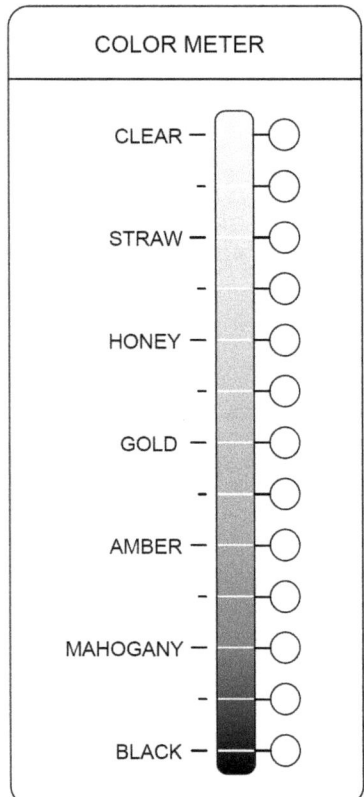

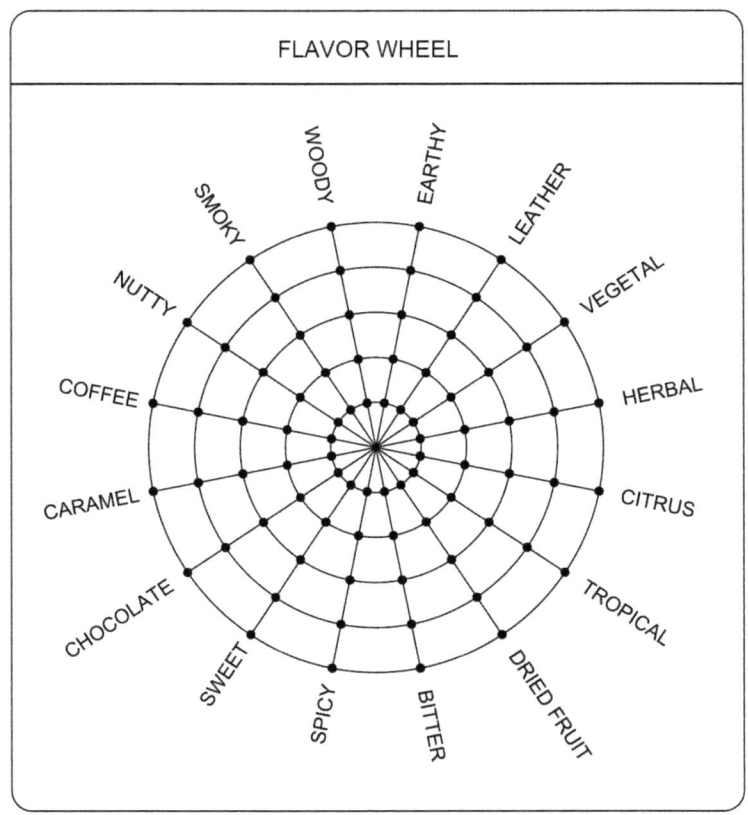

ADDITIONAL NOTES

FINAL RATING

- APPEARANCE ☆☆☆☆☆
- TASTE ☆☆☆☆☆
- MOUTHFEEL ☆☆☆☆☆
- OVERALL RATING ☆☆☆☆☆

	NAME		
	DISTILLERY		TYPE
	ORIGIN		AGE
	PRICE		SAMPLED

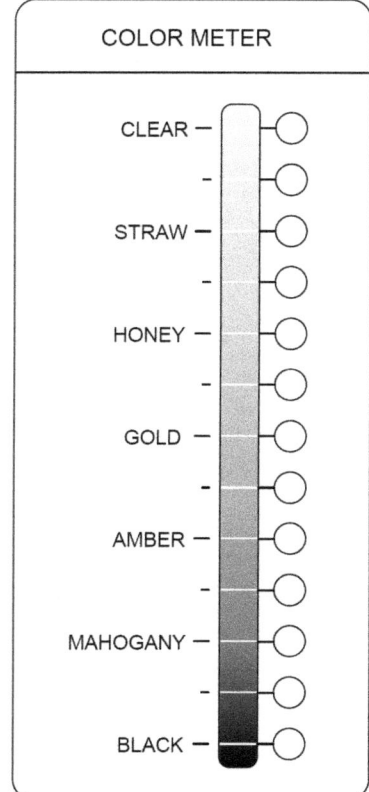

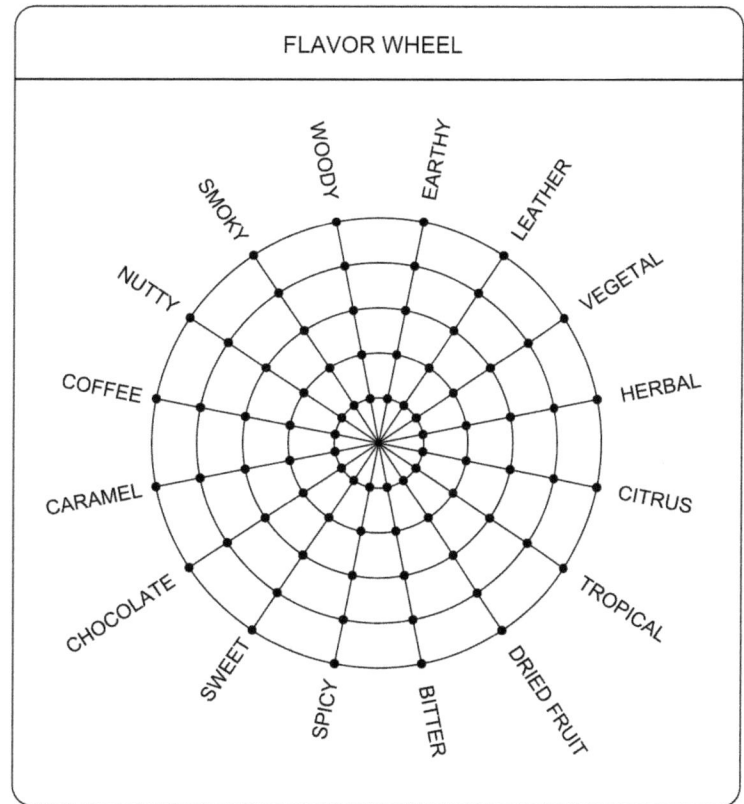

ADDITIONAL NOTES

FINAL RATING

- APPEARANCE ☆☆☆☆☆
- TASTE ☆☆☆☆☆
- MOUTHFEEL ☆☆☆☆☆
- OVERALL RATING ☆☆☆☆☆

🥃 NAME			
🏭 DISTILLERY		🍾 TYPE	
🌎 ORIGIN		🛢 AGE	
💰 PRICE		📅 SAMPLED	

COLOR METER

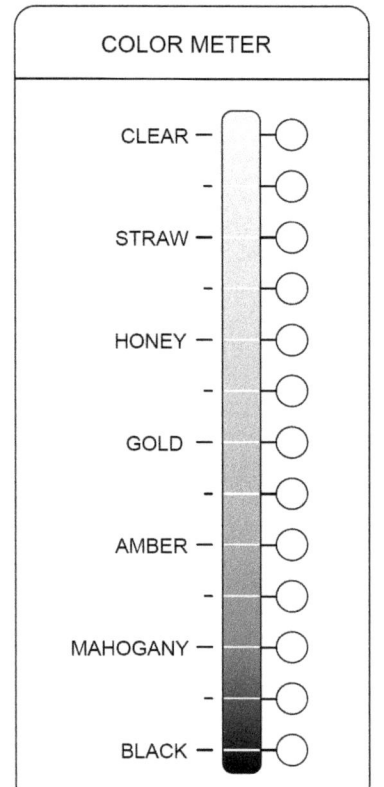

- CLEAR
- STRAW
- HONEY
- GOLD
- AMBER
- MAHOGANY
- BLACK

FLAVOR WHEEL

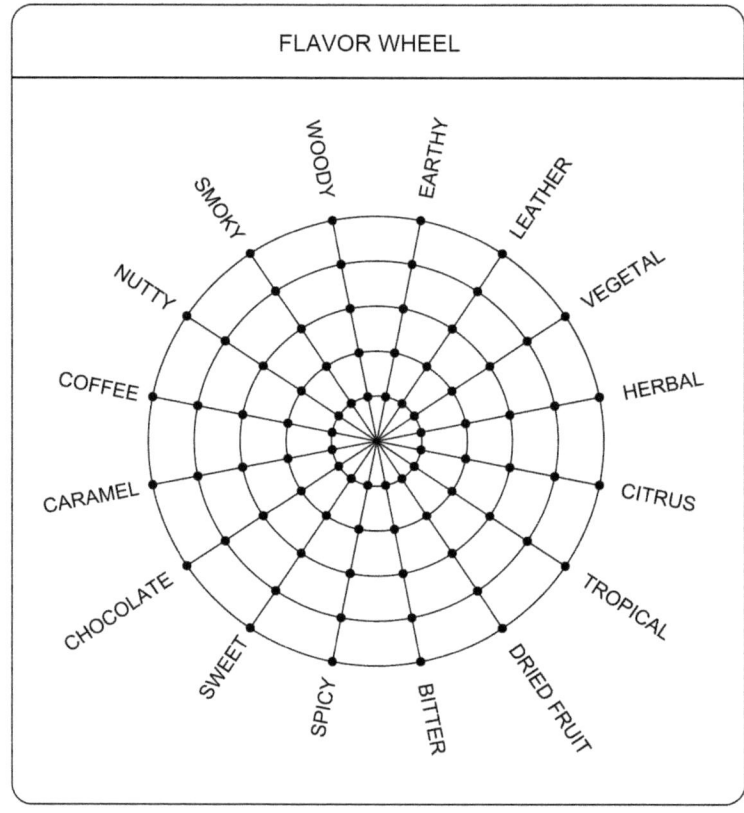

SMOKY, WOODY, EARTHY, LEATHER, VEGETAL, NUTTY, HERBAL, COFFEE, CITRUS, CARAMEL, TROPICAL, CHOCOLATE, DRIED FRUIT, SWEET, SPICY, BITTER

ADDITIONAL NOTES

FINAL RATING

- APPEARANCE ☆☆☆☆☆
- TASTE ☆☆☆☆☆
- MOUTHFEEL ☆☆☆☆☆
- OVERALL RATING ☆☆☆☆☆

	NAME		
	DISTILLERY		TYPE
	ORIGIN		AGE
	PRICE		SAMPLED

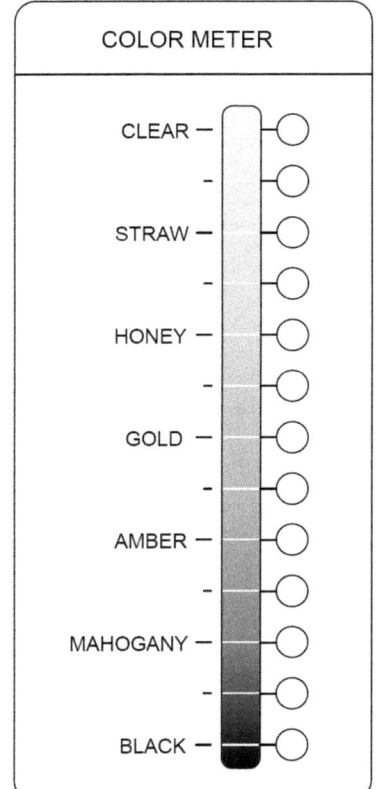

COLOR METER

- CLEAR
- STRAW
- HONEY
- GOLD
- AMBER
- MAHOGANY
- BLACK

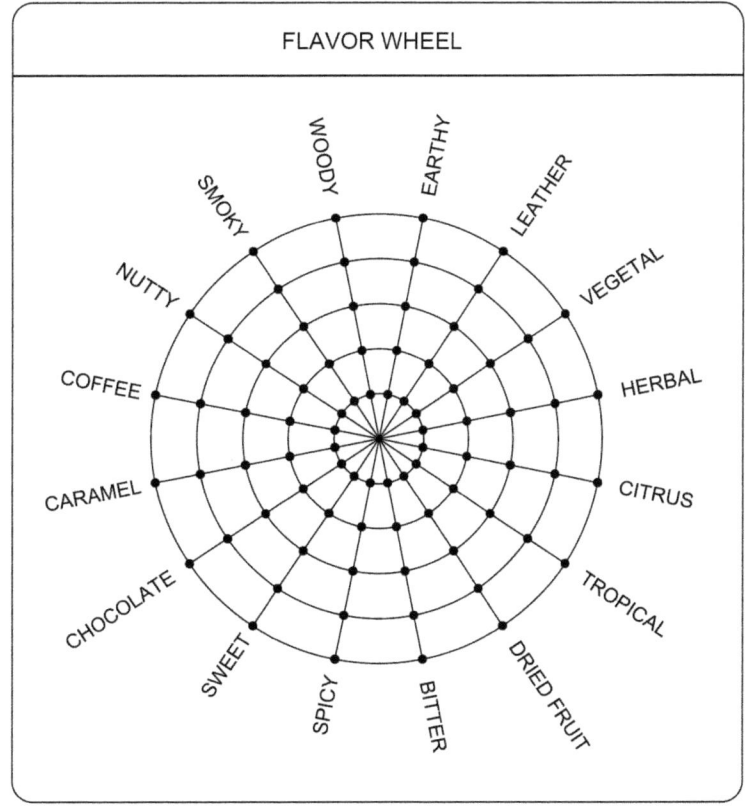

FLAVOR WHEEL

SMOKY, WOODY, EARTHY, LEATHER, VEGETAL, HERBAL, CITRUS, TROPICAL, DRIED FRUIT, BITTER, SPICY, SWEET, CHOCOLATE, CARAMEL, COFFEE, NUTTY

ADDITIONAL NOTES

FINAL RATING

- APPEARANCE ☆☆☆☆☆
- TASTE ☆☆☆☆☆
- MOUTHFEEL ☆☆☆☆☆
- OVERALL RATING ☆☆☆☆☆

NAME	
DISTILLERY	TYPE
ORIGIN	AGE
PRICE	SAMPLED

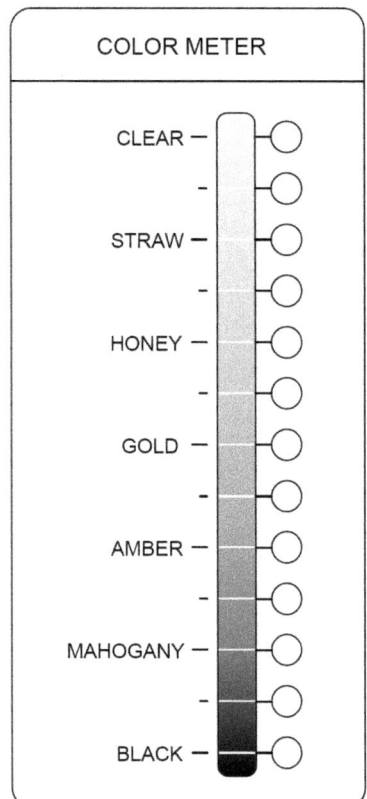

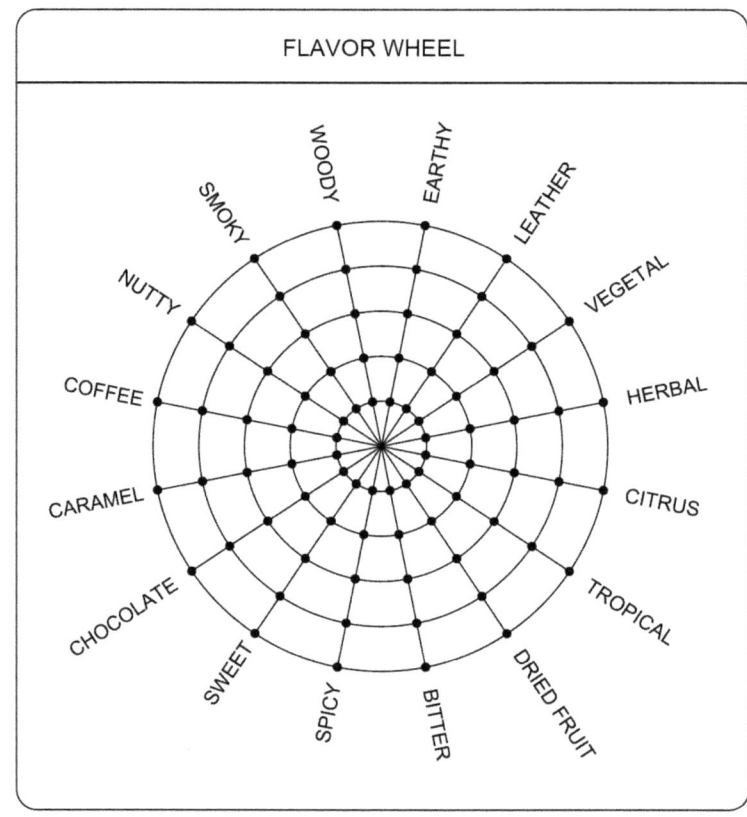

ADDITIONAL NOTES

FINAL RATING

- APPEARANCE ☆☆☆☆☆
- TASTE ☆☆☆☆☆
- MOUTHFEEL ☆☆☆☆☆
- OVERALL RATING ☆☆☆☆☆

NAME			
DISTILLERY		TYPE	
ORIGIN		AGE	
PRICE		SAMPLED	

COLOR METER

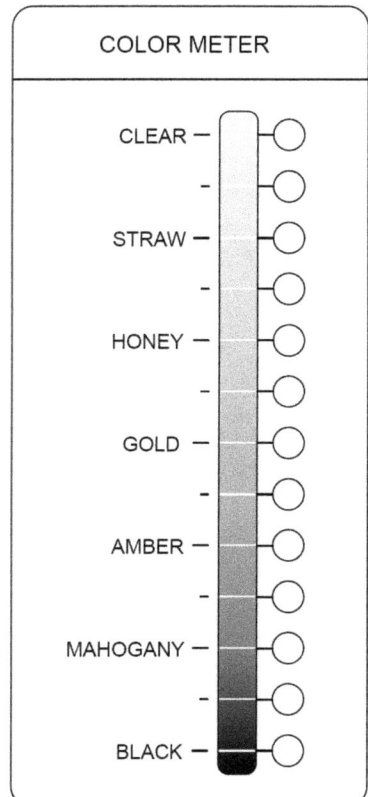

- CLEAR
- STRAW
- HONEY
- GOLD
- AMBER
- MAHOGANY
- BLACK

FLAVOR WHEEL

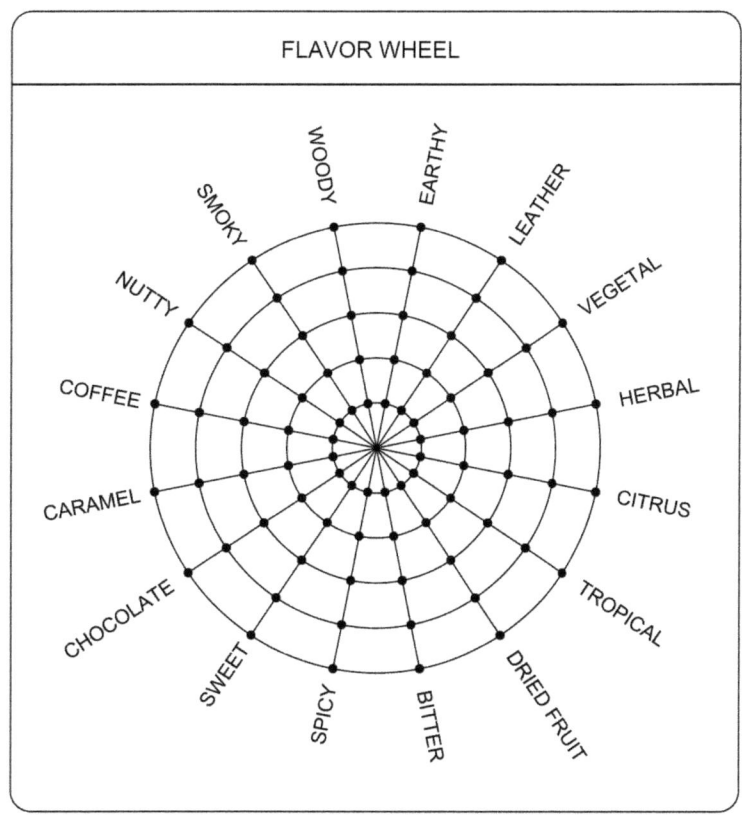

SMOKY, WOODY, EARTHY, LEATHER, NUTTY, VEGETAL, COFFEE, HERBAL, CARAMEL, CITRUS, CHOCOLATE, TROPICAL, SWEET, SPICY, BITTER, DRIED FRUIT

ADDITIONAL NOTES

FINAL RATING

- APPEARANCE ☆☆☆☆☆
- TASTE ☆☆☆☆☆
- MOUTHFEEL ☆☆☆☆☆
- OVERALL RATING ☆☆☆☆☆

	NAME		
	DISTILLERY		TYPE
	ORIGIN		AGE
	PRICE		SAMPLED

COLOR METER

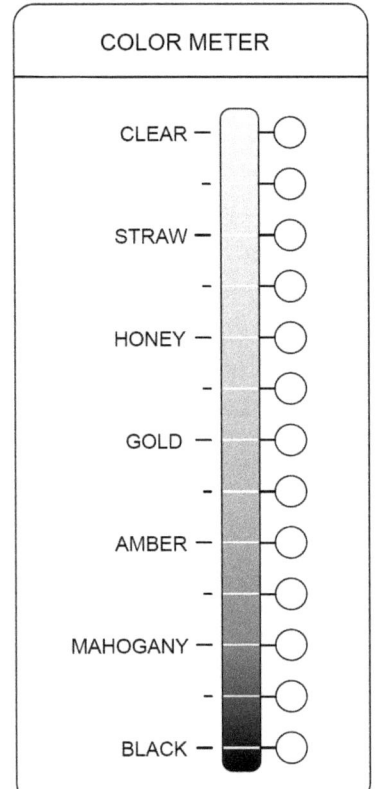

- CLEAR
- STRAW
- HONEY
- GOLD
- AMBER
- MAHOGANY
- BLACK

FLAVOR WHEEL

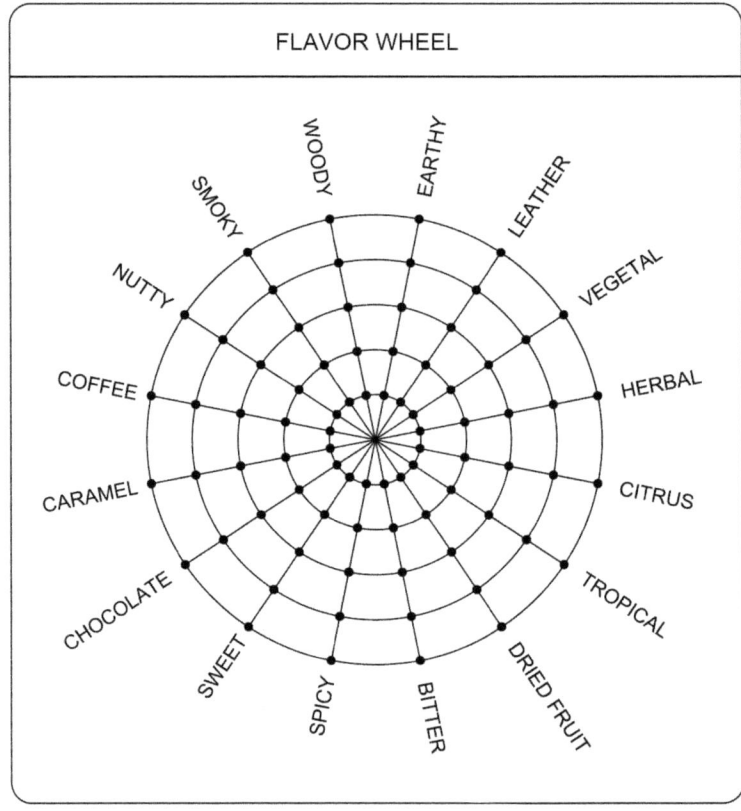

SMOKY, WOODY, EARTHY, LEATHER, VEGETAL, HERBAL, CITRUS, TROPICAL, DRIED FRUIT, BITTER, SPICY, SWEET, CHOCOLATE, CARAMEL, COFFEE, NUTTY

ADDITIONAL NOTES

FINAL RATING

- APPEARANCE ☆☆☆☆☆
- TASTE ☆☆☆☆☆
- MOUTHFEEL ☆☆☆☆☆
- OVERALL RATING ☆☆☆☆☆

	NAME		
	DISTILLERY		TYPE
	ORIGIN		AGE
	PRICE		SAMPLED

COLOR METER

- CLEAR
- STRAW
- HONEY
- GOLD
- AMBER
- MAHOGANY
- BLACK

FLAVOR WHEEL

SMOKY, WOODY, EARTHY, LEATHER, VEGETAL, NUTTY, HERBAL, COFFEE, CITRUS, CARAMEL, TROPICAL, CHOCOLATE, DRIED FRUIT, SWEET, SPICY, BITTER

ADDITIONAL NOTES

FINAL RATING

- APPEARANCE ☆☆☆☆☆
- TASTE ☆☆☆☆☆
- MOUTHFEEL ☆☆☆☆☆
- OVERALL RATING ☆☆☆☆☆

🥃 NAME			
⚗️ DISTILLERY		🍾 TYPE	
🌍 ORIGIN		🛢️ AGE	
💰 PRICE		📅 SAMPLED	

COLOR METER

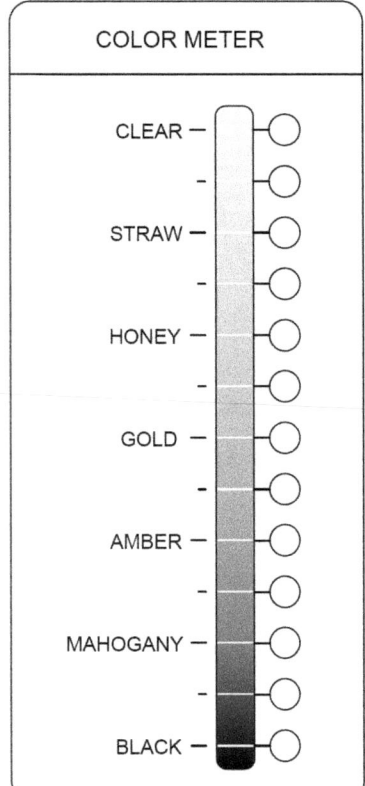

- CLEAR
- STRAW
- HONEY
- GOLD
- AMBER
- MAHOGANY
- BLACK

FLAVOR WHEEL

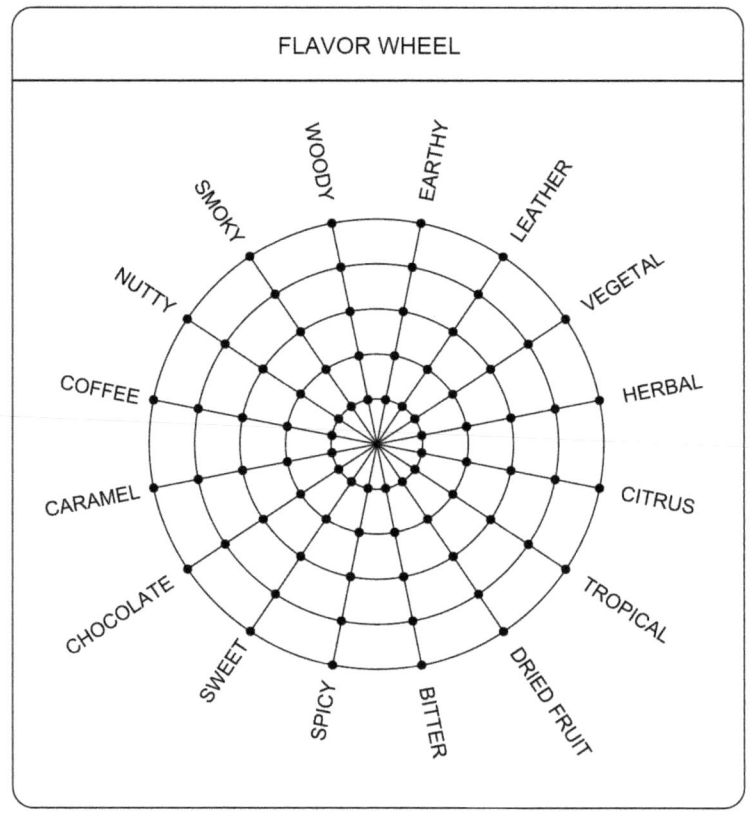

SMOKY, WOODY, EARTHY, LEATHER, VEGETAL, HERBAL, CITRUS, TROPICAL, DRIED FRUIT, BITTER, SPICY, SWEET, CHOCOLATE, CARAMEL, COFFEE, NUTTY

ADDITIONAL NOTES

FINAL RATING

- APPEARANCE ☆☆☆☆☆
- TASTE ☆☆☆☆☆
- MOUTHFEEL ☆☆☆☆☆
- OVERALL RATING ☆☆☆☆☆

	NAME		
	DISTILLERY		TYPE
	ORIGIN		AGE
	PRICE		SAMPLED

COLOR METER

- CLEAR
- STRAW
- HONEY
- GOLD
- AMBER
- MAHOGANY
- BLACK

FLAVOR WHEEL

SMOKY, WOODY, EARTHY, LEATHER, VEGETAL, HERBAL, CITRUS, TROPICAL, DRIED FRUIT, BITTER, SPICY, SWEET, CHOCOLATE, CARAMEL, COFFEE, NUTTY

ADDITIONAL NOTES

FINAL RATING

- APPEARANCE ☆☆☆☆☆
- TASTE ☆☆☆☆☆
- MOUTHFEEL ☆☆☆☆☆
- OVERALL RATING ☆☆☆☆☆

🥃 NAME			
🍾 DISTILLERY		🍶 TYPE	
🌍 ORIGIN		🛢 AGE	
💰 PRICE		📅 SAMPLED	

COLOR METER

- CLEAR
- STRAW
- HONEY
- GOLD
- AMBER
- MAHOGANY
- BLACK

FLAVOR WHEEL

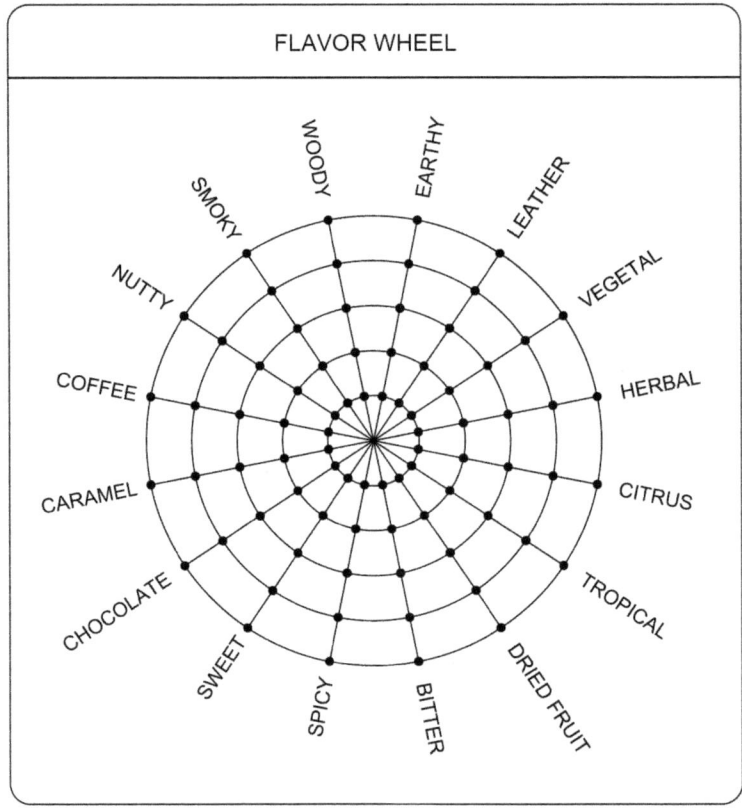

Flavors: WOODY, EARTHY, SMOKY, LEATHER, NUTTY, VEGETAL, COFFEE, HERBAL, CARAMEL, CITRUS, CHOCOLATE, TROPICAL, SWEET, SPICY, BITTER, DRIED FRUIT

ADDITIONAL NOTES

FINAL RATING

- APPEARANCE ☆☆☆☆☆
- TASTE ☆☆☆☆☆
- MOUTHFEEL ☆☆☆☆☆
- OVERALL RATING ☆☆☆☆☆

	NAME		
	DISTILLERY		TYPE
	ORIGIN		AGE
	PRICE		SAMPLED

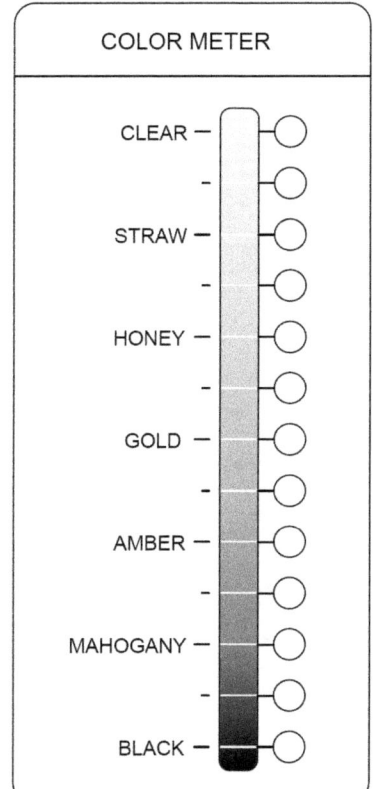

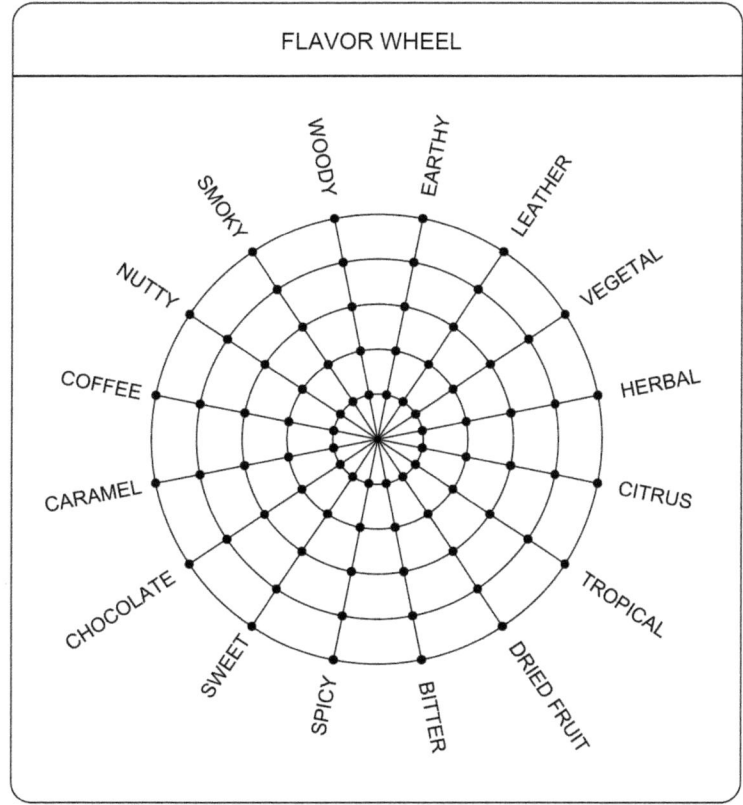

ADDITIONAL NOTES

FINAL RATING

- APPEARANCE ☆☆☆☆☆
- TASTE ☆☆☆☆☆
- MOUTHFEEL ☆☆☆☆☆
- OVERALL RATING ☆☆☆☆☆

	NAME		
	DISTILLERY		TYPE
	ORIGIN		AGE
	PRICE		SAMPLED

COLOR METER

- CLEAR
- —
- STRAW
- —
- HONEY
- —
- GOLD
- —
- AMBER
- —
- MAHOGANY
- —
- BLACK

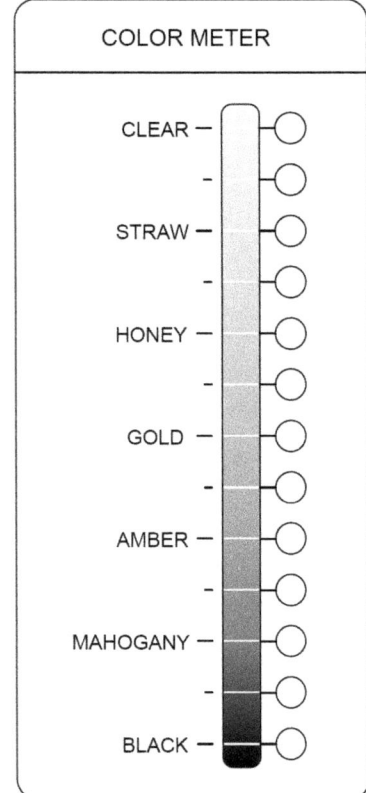

FLAVOR WHEEL

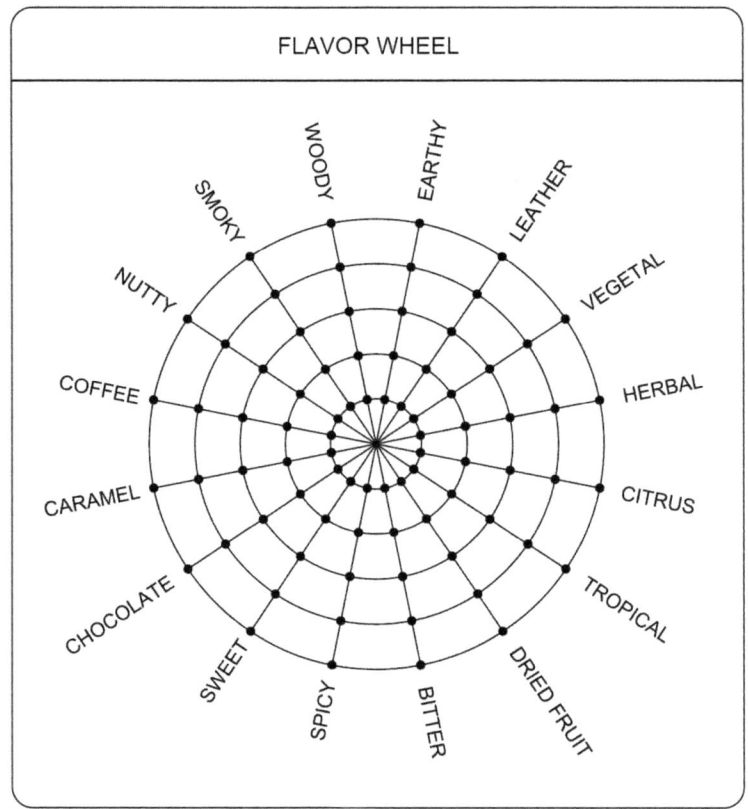

SMOKY · WOODY · EARTHY · LEATHER · VEGETAL · HERBAL · CITRUS · TROPICAL · DRIED FRUIT · BITTER · SPICY · SWEET · CHOCOLATE · CARAMEL · COFFEE · NUTTY

ADDITIONAL NOTES

FINAL RATING

- APPEARANCE ☆☆☆☆☆
- TASTE ☆☆☆☆☆
- MOUTHFEEL ☆☆☆☆☆
- OVERALL RATING ☆☆☆☆☆

	NAME		
	DISTILLERY		TYPE
	ORIGIN		AGE
	PRICE		SAMPLED

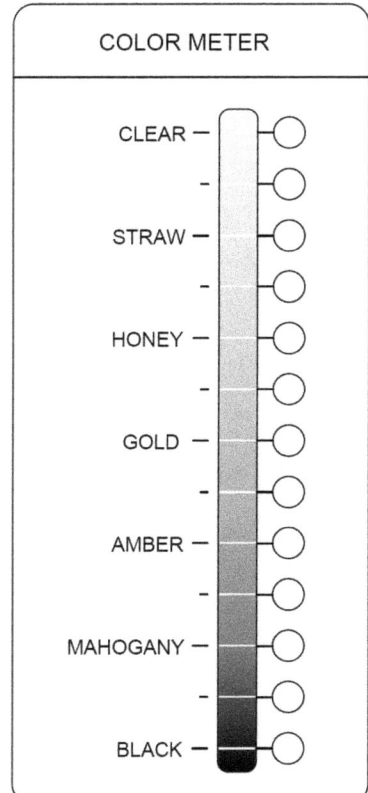

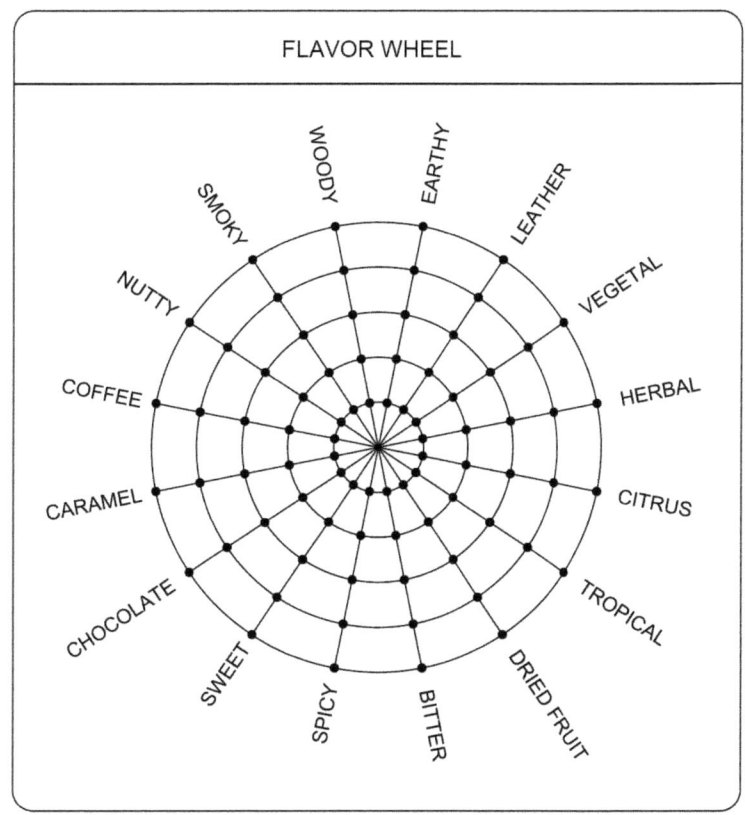

ADDITIONAL NOTES

FINAL RATING

- APPEARANCE ☆☆☆☆☆
- TASTE ☆☆☆☆☆
- MOUTHFEEL ☆☆☆☆☆
- OVERALL RATING ☆☆☆☆☆

	NAME		
	DISTILLERY		TYPE
	ORIGIN		AGE
	PRICE		SAMPLED

COLOR METER

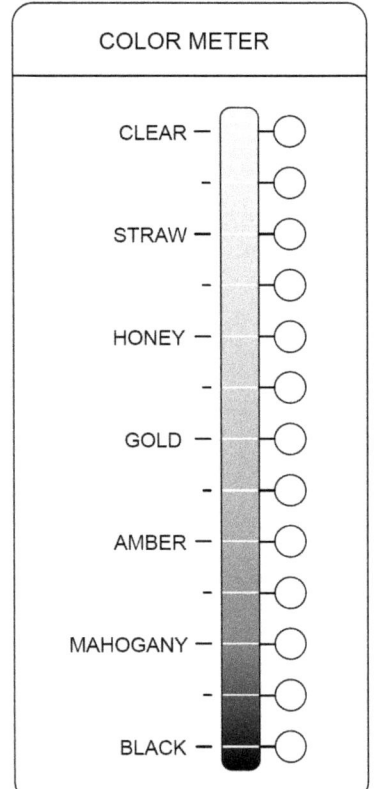

- CLEAR
- STRAW
- HONEY
- GOLD
- AMBER
- MAHOGANY
- BLACK

FLAVOR WHEEL

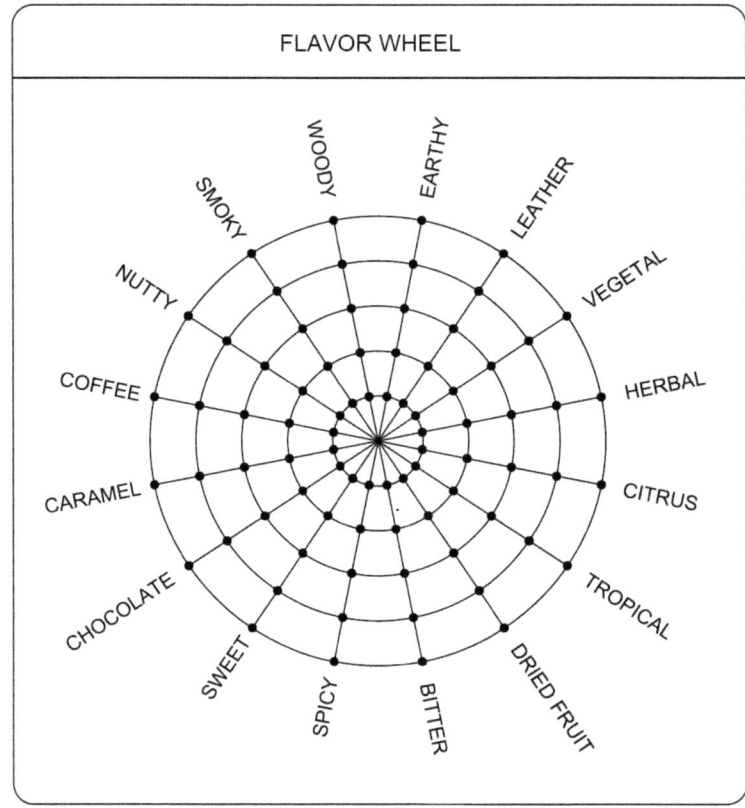

SMOKY, WOODY, EARTHY, LEATHER, NUTTY, VEGETAL, COFFEE, HERBAL, CARAMEL, CITRUS, CHOCOLATE, TROPICAL, SWEET, SPICY, BITTER, DRIED FRUIT

ADDITIONAL NOTES

FINAL RATING

- APPEARANCE ☆☆☆☆☆
- TASTE ☆☆☆☆☆
- MOUTHFEEL ☆☆☆☆☆
- OVERALL RATING ☆☆☆☆☆

	NAME		
	DISTILLERY		TYPE
	ORIGIN		AGE
	PRICE		SAMPLED

COLOR METER

- CLEAR
- STRAW
- HONEY
- GOLD
- AMBER
- MAHOGANY
- BLACK

FLAVOR WHEEL

SMOKY, WOODY, EARTHY, LEATHER, VEGETAL, HERBAL, CITRUS, TROPICAL, DRIED FRUIT, BITTER, SPICY, SWEET, CHOCOLATE, CARAMEL, COFFEE, NUTTY

ADDITIONAL NOTES

FINAL RATING

- APPEARANCE ☆☆☆☆☆
- TASTE ☆☆☆☆☆
- MOUTHFEEL ☆☆☆☆☆
- OVERALL RATING ☆☆☆☆☆

🥃 NAME			
🏭 DISTILLERY		🍾 TYPE	
🌍 ORIGIN		🛢 AGE	
💵 PRICE		📅 SAMPLED	

COLOR METER

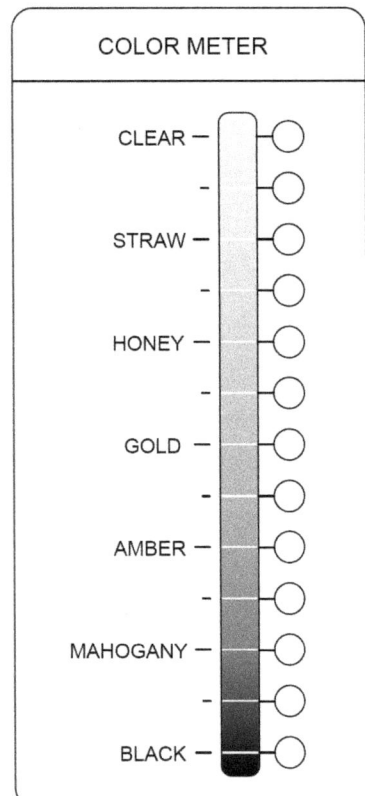

- CLEAR
- STRAW
- HONEY
- GOLD
- AMBER
- MAHOGANY
- BLACK

FLAVOR WHEEL

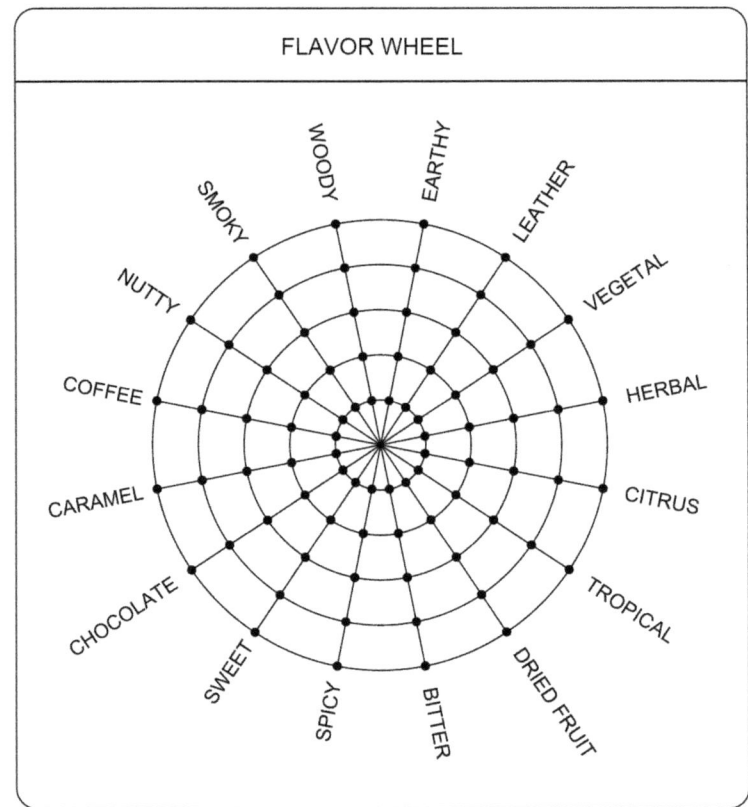

SMOKY, WOODY, EARTHY, LEATHER, NUTTY, VEGETAL, COFFEE, HERBAL, CARAMEL, CITRUS, CHOCOLATE, TROPICAL, SWEET, SPICY, BITTER, DRIED FRUIT

ADDITIONAL NOTES

FINAL RATING

- 🍾 APPEARANCE ☆☆☆☆☆
- 🌾 TASTE ☆☆☆☆☆
- 👄 MOUTHFEEL ☆☆☆☆☆
- ⭐ OVERALL RATING ☆☆☆☆☆

	NAME		
	DISTILLERY		TYPE
	ORIGIN		AGE
	PRICE		SAMPLED

COLOR METER

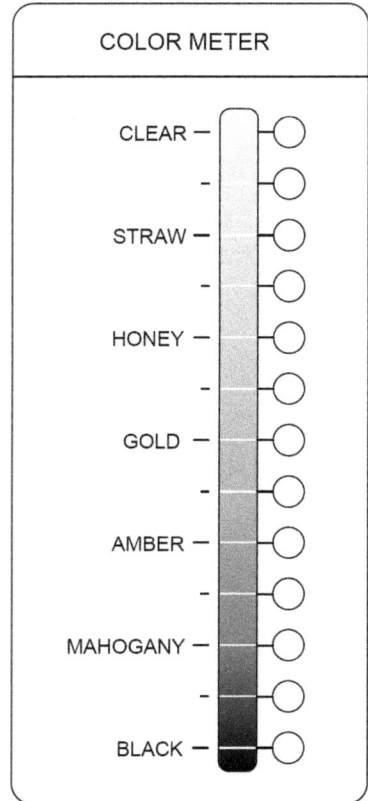

- CLEAR
- STRAW
- HONEY
- GOLD
- AMBER
- MAHOGANY
- BLACK

FLAVOR WHEEL

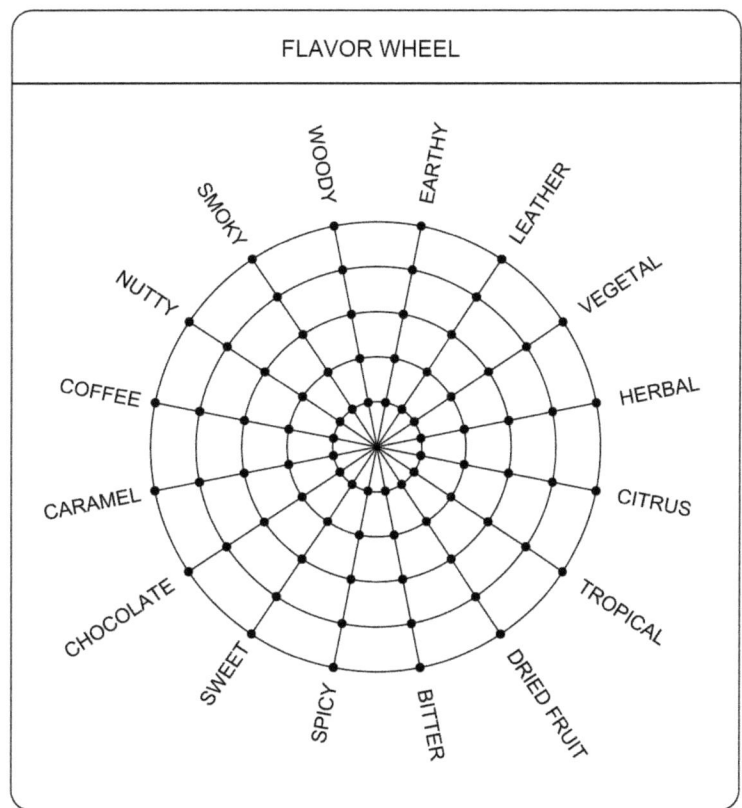

SMOKY, WOODY, EARTHY, LEATHER, VEGETAL, HERBAL, CITRUS, TROPICAL, DRIED FRUIT, BITTER, SPICY, SWEET, CHOCOLATE, CARAMEL, COFFEE, NUTTY

ADDITIONAL NOTES

FINAL RATING

- APPEARANCE ☆☆☆☆☆
- TASTE ☆☆☆☆☆
- MOUTHFEEL ☆☆☆☆☆
- OVERALL RATING ☆☆☆☆☆

NAME			
DISTILLERY		TYPE	
ORIGIN		AGE	
PRICE		SAMPLED	

COLOR METER

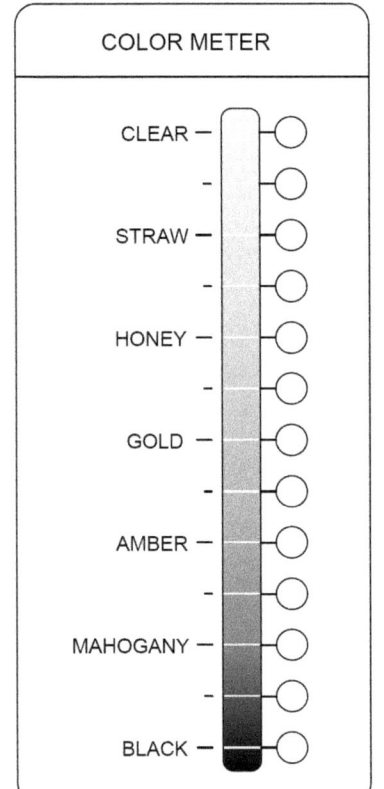

- CLEAR
- STRAW
- HONEY
- GOLD
- AMBER
- MAHOGANY
- BLACK

FLAVOR WHEEL

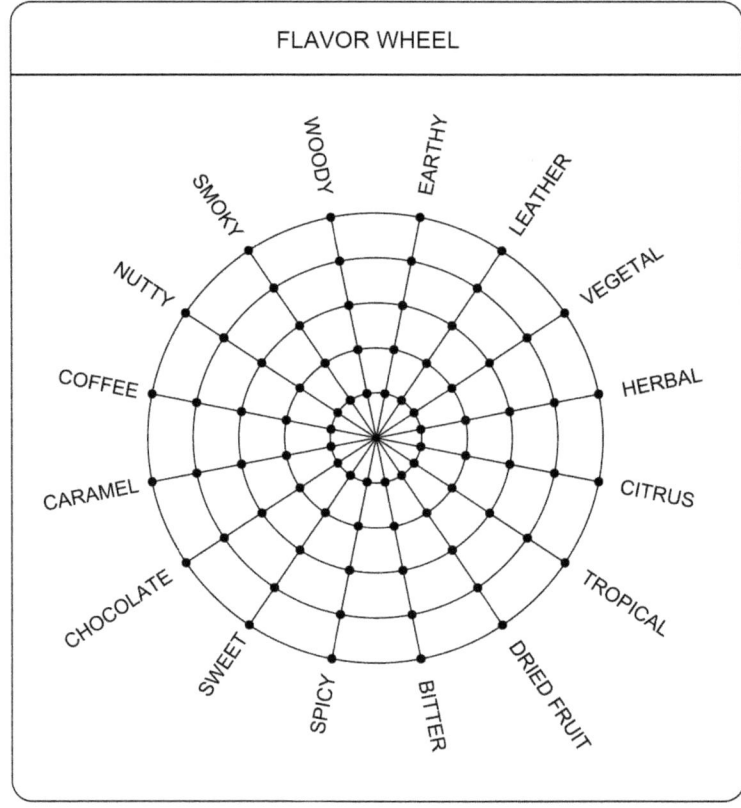

SMOKY, WOODY, EARTHY, LEATHER, VEGETAL, HERBAL, CITRUS, TROPICAL, DRIED FRUIT, BITTER, SPICY, SWEET, CHOCOLATE, CARAMEL, COFFEE, NUTTY

ADDITIONAL NOTES

FINAL RATING

- APPEARANCE ☆☆☆☆☆
- TASTE ☆☆☆☆☆
- MOUTHFEEL ☆☆☆☆☆
- OVERALL RATING ☆☆☆☆☆

	NAME		
	DISTILLERY		TYPE
	ORIGIN		AGE
	PRICE		SAMPLED

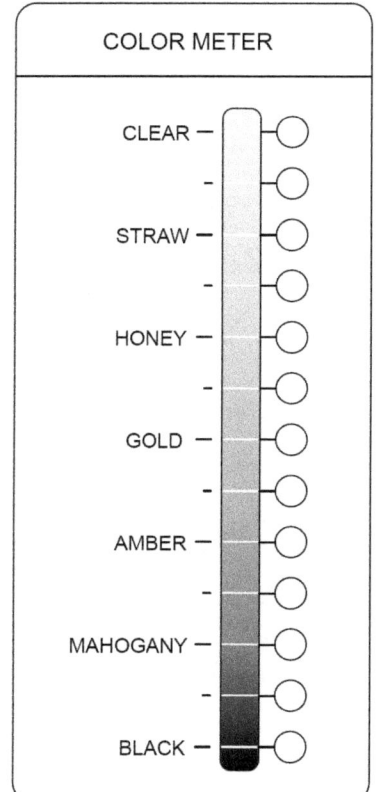

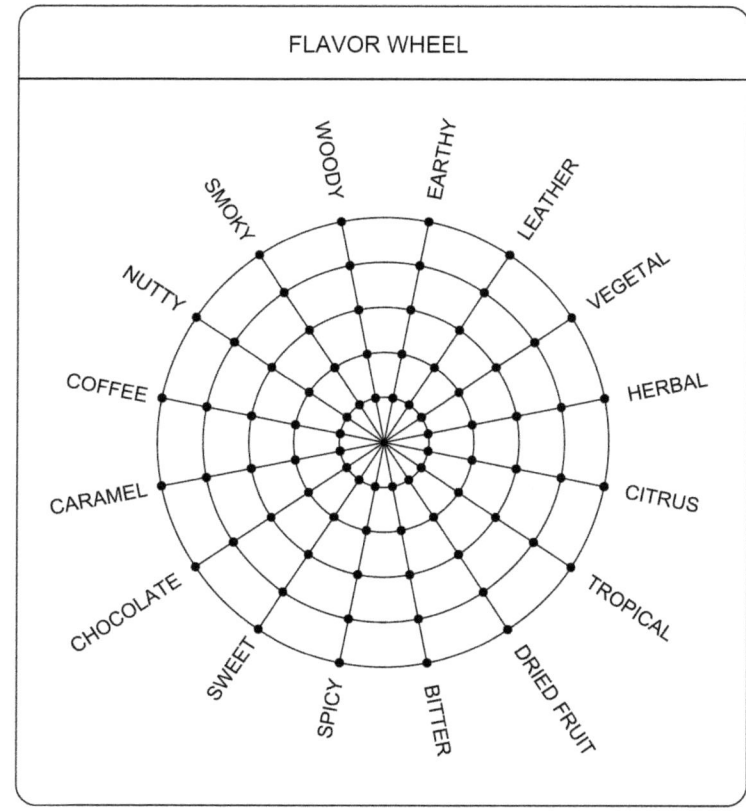

ADDITIONAL NOTES

FINAL RATING

- APPEARANCE ☆☆☆☆☆
- TASTE ☆☆☆☆☆
- MOUTHFEEL ☆☆☆☆☆
- OVERALL RATING ☆☆☆☆☆

🥃 NAME			
🛢 DISTILLERY		🍾 TYPE	
🌐 ORIGIN		🛢 AGE	
💰 PRICE		📅 SAMPLED	

COLOR METER

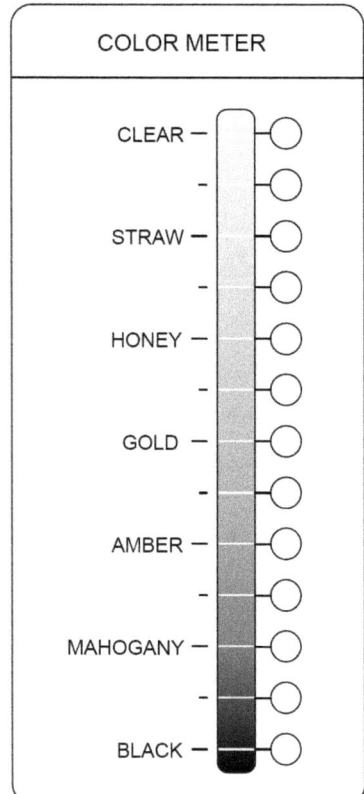

FLAVOR WHEEL

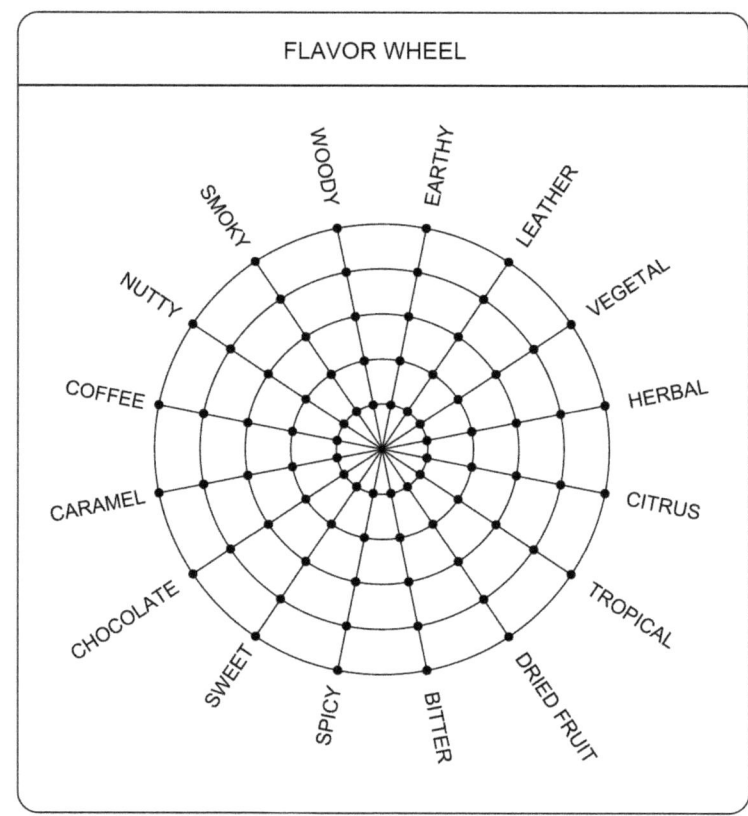

ADDITIONAL NOTES

FINAL RATING

- APPEARANCE ☆☆☆☆☆
- TASTE ☆☆☆☆☆
- MOUTHFEEL ☆☆☆☆☆
- OVERALL RATING ☆☆☆☆☆

NAME	

DISTILLERY		TYPE	
ORIGIN		AGE	
PRICE		SAMPLED	

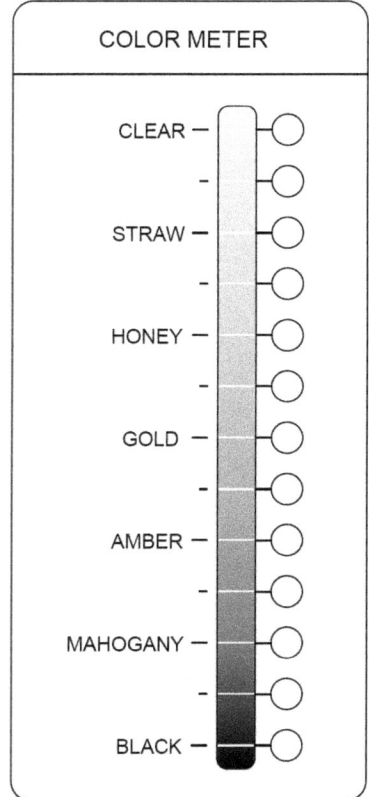

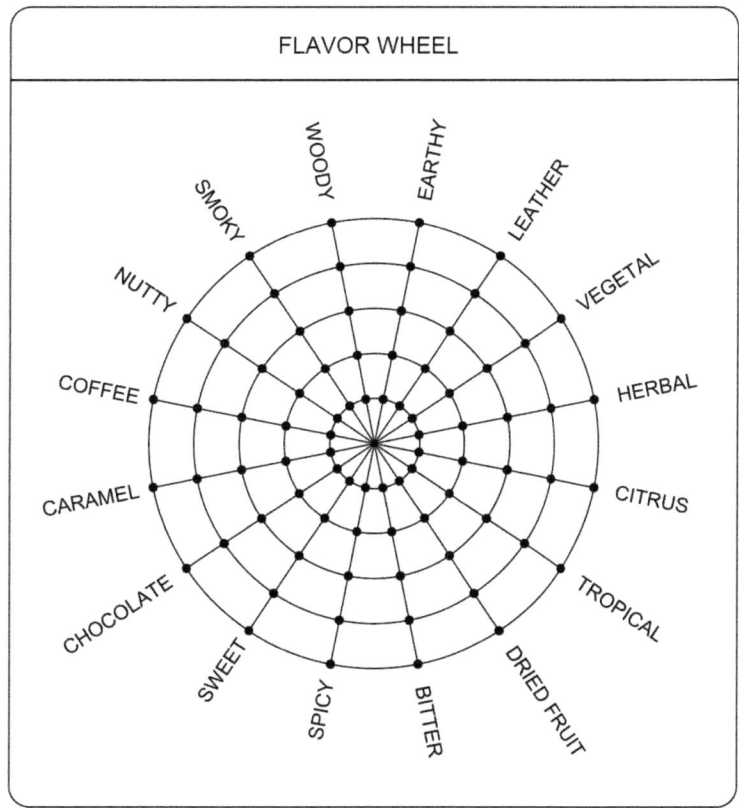

ADDITIONAL NOTES

FINAL RATING

- APPEARANCE ☆☆☆☆☆
- TASTE ☆☆☆☆☆
- MOUTHFEEL ☆☆☆☆☆
- OVERALL RATING ☆☆☆☆☆

	NAME		
	DISTILLERY		TYPE
	ORIGIN		AGE
	PRICE		SAMPLED

COLOR METER

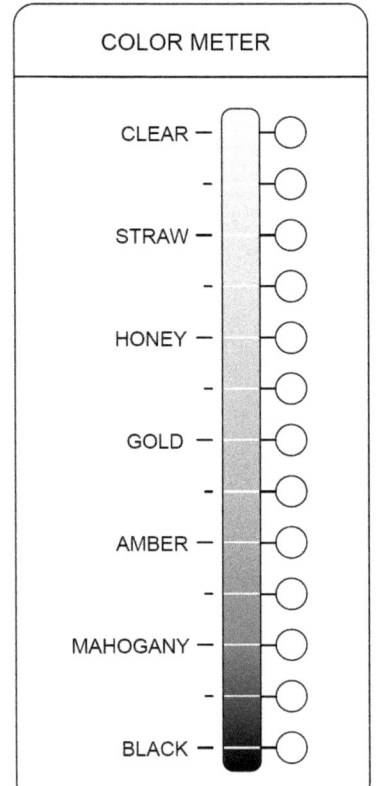

- CLEAR
- STRAW
- HONEY
- GOLD
- AMBER
- MAHOGANY
- BLACK

FLAVOR WHEEL

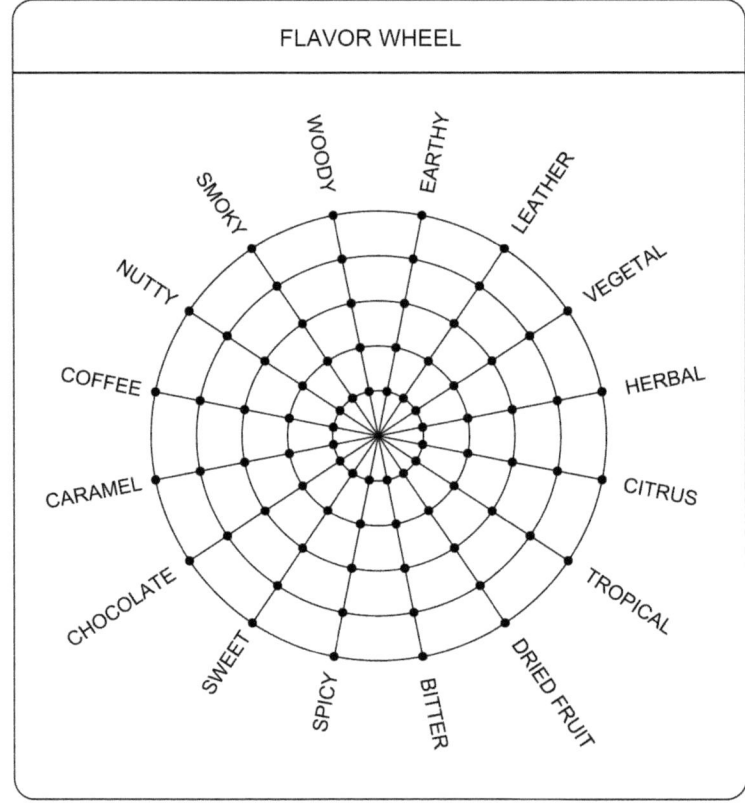

SMOKY · WOODY · EARTHY · LEATHER · VEGETAL · HERBAL · CITRUS · TROPICAL · DRIED FRUIT · BITTER · SPICY · SWEET · CHOCOLATE · CARAMEL · COFFEE · NUTTY

ADDITIONAL NOTES

FINAL RATING

- APPEARANCE ☆☆☆☆☆
- TASTE ☆☆☆☆☆
- MOUTHFEEL ☆☆☆☆☆
- OVERALL RATING ☆☆☆☆☆

	NAME		
	DISTILLERY		TYPE
	ORIGIN		AGE
	PRICE		SAMPLED

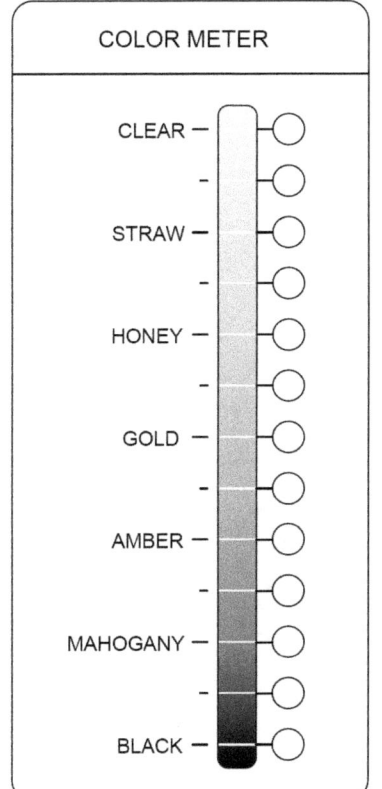

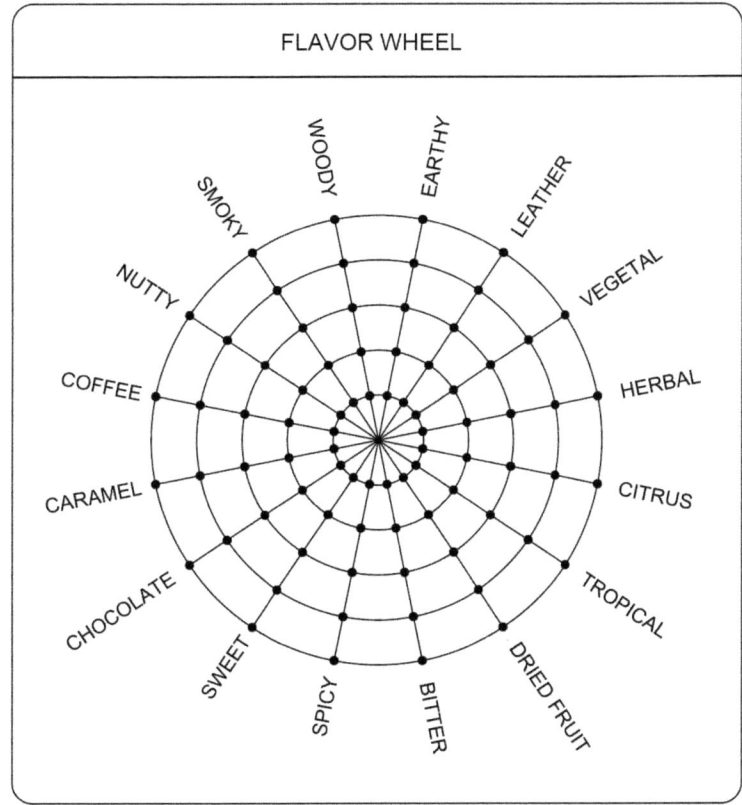

ADDITIONAL NOTES

FINAL RATING

- APPEARANCE ☆☆☆☆☆
- TASTE ☆☆☆☆☆
- MOUTHFEEL ☆☆☆☆☆
- OVERALL RATING ☆☆☆☆☆

🥃 NAME	
🛢 DISTILLERY	🍾 TYPE
🌍 ORIGIN	🛢 AGE
💰 PRICE	📅 SAMPLED

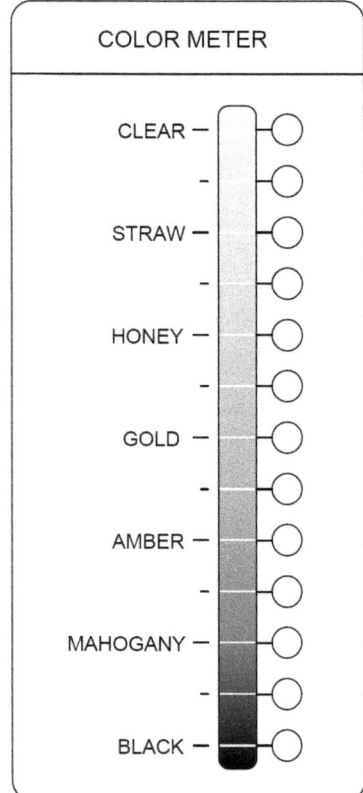

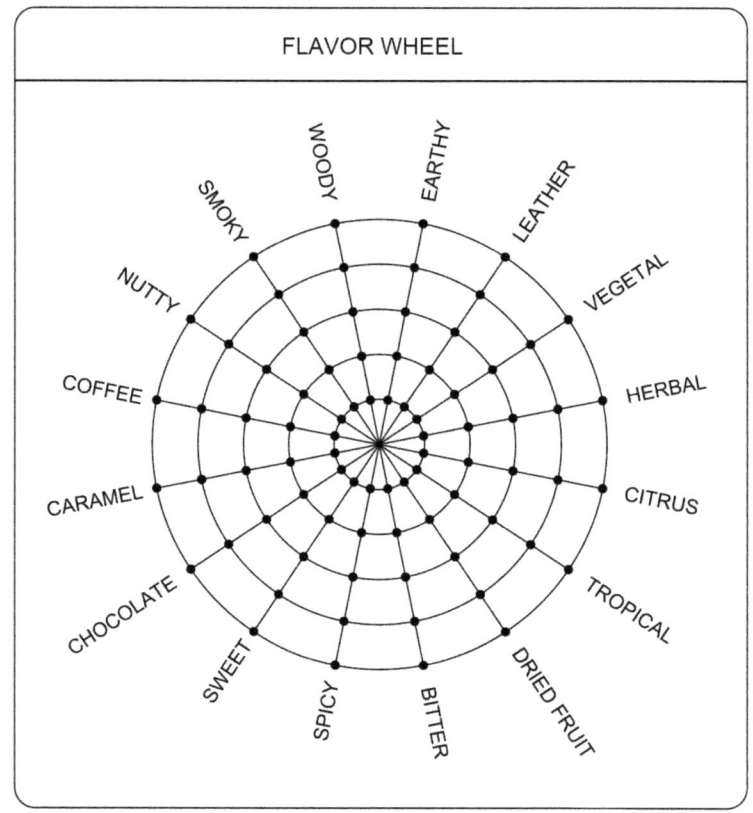

ADDITIONAL NOTES

FINAL RATING

- APPEARANCE ☆☆☆☆☆
- TASTE ☆☆☆☆☆
- MOUTHFEEL ☆☆☆☆☆
- OVERALL RATING ☆☆☆☆☆

	NAME		
	DISTILLERY		TYPE
	ORIGIN		AGE
	PRICE		SAMPLED

COLOR METER

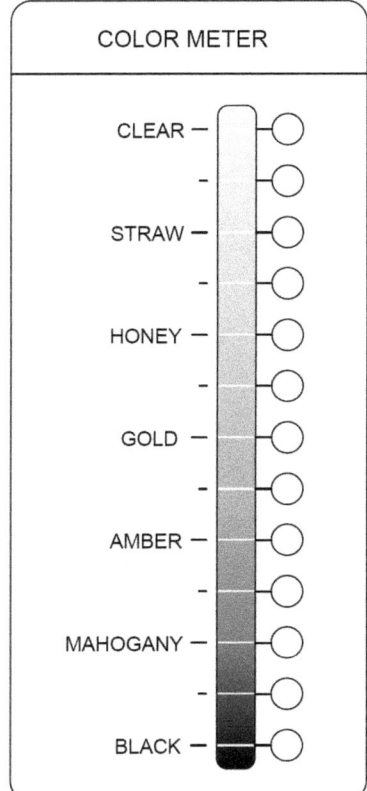

- CLEAR
- STRAW
- HONEY
- GOLD
- AMBER
- MAHOGANY
- BLACK

FLAVOR WHEEL

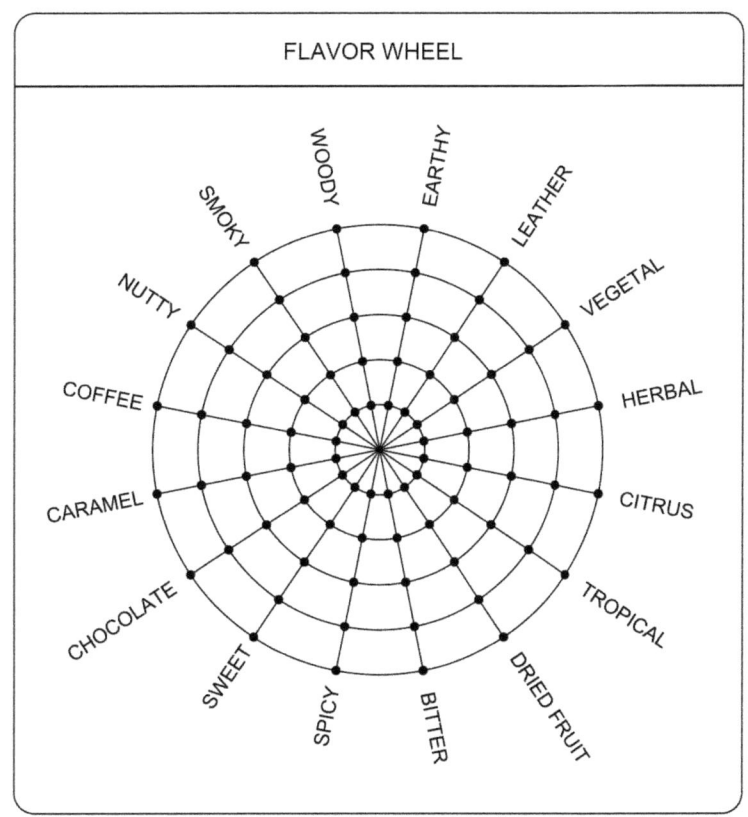

SMOKY, WOODY, EARTHY, LEATHER, NUTTY, VEGETAL, COFFEE, HERBAL, CARAMEL, CITRUS, CHOCOLATE, TROPICAL, SWEET, SPICY, BITTER, DRIED FRUIT

ADDITIONAL NOTES

FINAL RATING

- APPEARANCE ☆☆☆☆☆
- TASTE ☆☆☆☆☆
- MOUTHFEEL ☆☆☆☆☆
- OVERALL RATING ☆☆☆☆☆

🥃 NAME	
🍾 DISTILLERY	🍶 TYPE
🌍 ORIGIN	🛢 AGE
💲 PRICE	📅 SAMPLED

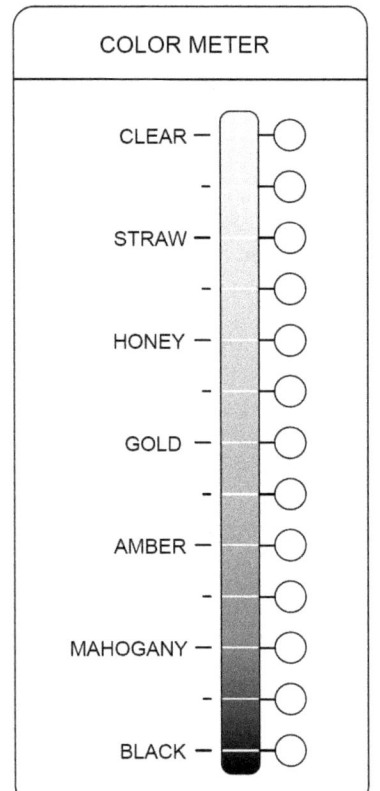

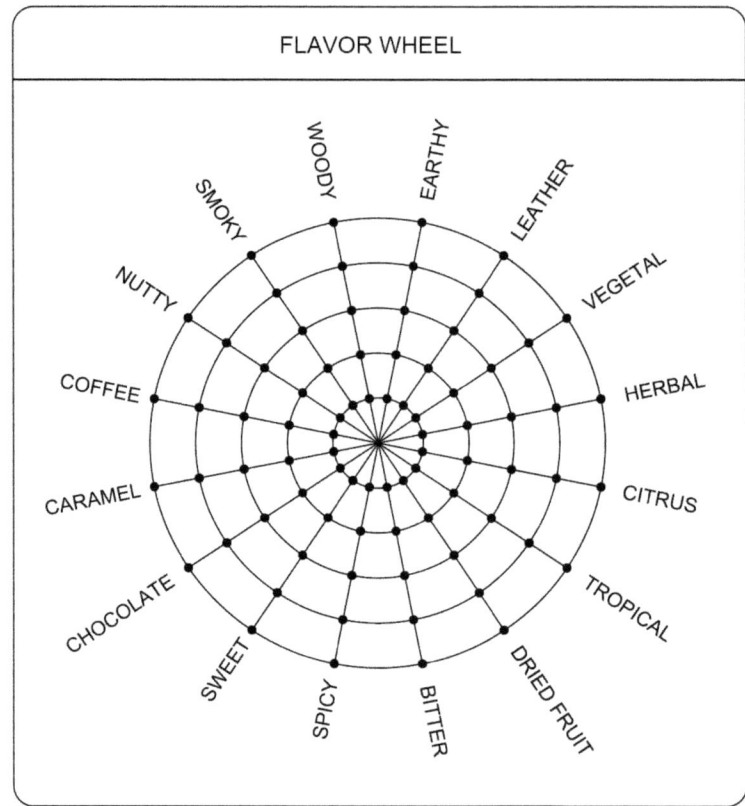

ADDITIONAL NOTES

_____

_____

FINAL RATING

🍾 APPEARANCE	☆☆☆☆☆	_____
🌾 TASTE	☆☆☆☆☆	_____
👄 MOUTHFEEL	☆☆☆☆☆	_____
🖐 OVERALL RATING	☆☆☆☆☆	_____

	NAME		
	DISTILLERY		TYPE
	ORIGIN		AGE
	PRICE		SAMPLED

COLOR METER

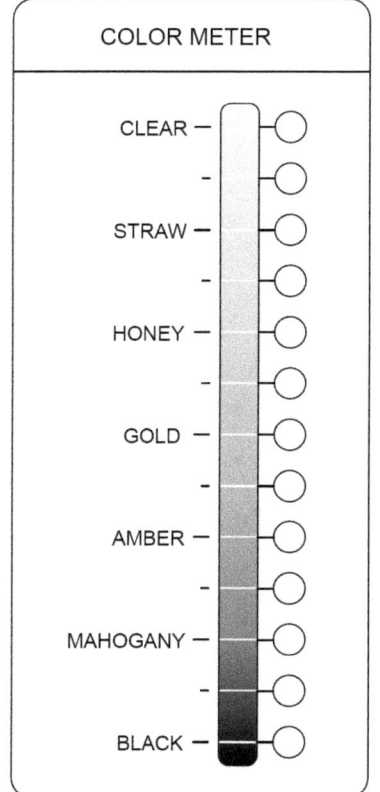

- CLEAR
- STRAW
- HONEY
- GOLD
- AMBER
- MAHOGANY
- BLACK

FLAVOR WHEEL

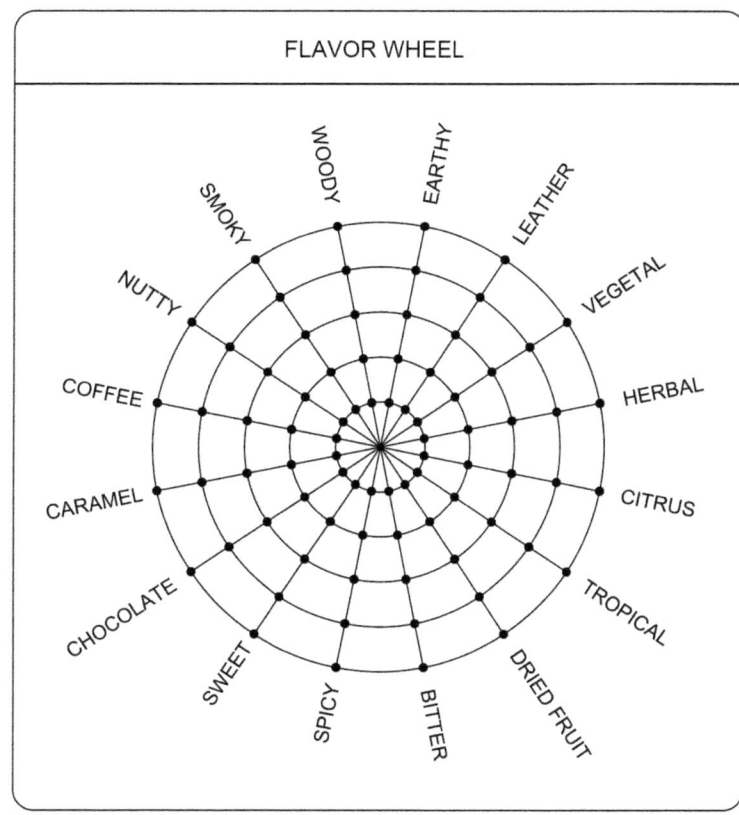

SMOKY · WOODY · EARTHY · LEATHER · VEGETAL · HERBAL · CITRUS · TROPICAL · DRIED FRUIT · BITTER · SPICY · SWEET · CHOCOLATE · CARAMEL · COFFEE · NUTTY

ADDITIONAL NOTES

FINAL RATING

- APPEARANCE ☆☆☆☆☆
- TASTE ☆☆☆☆☆
- MOUTHFEEL ☆☆☆☆☆
- OVERALL RATING ☆☆☆☆☆

🥃 NAME			
🛢️ DISTILLERY		🍾 TYPE	
🌍 ORIGIN		🛢️ AGE	
💲 PRICE		📅 SAMPLED	

COLOR METER

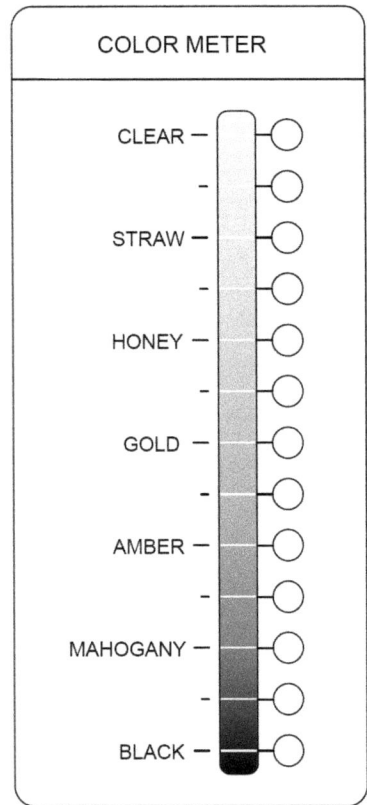

- CLEAR
- STRAW
- HONEY
- GOLD
- AMBER
- MAHOGANY
- BLACK

FLAVOR WHEEL

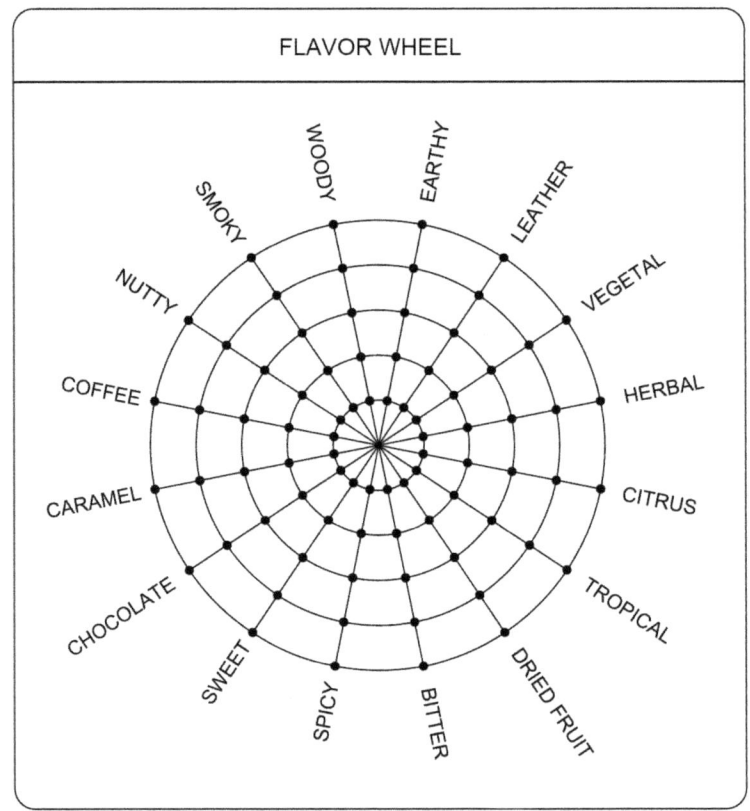

WOODY, EARTHY, LEATHER, VEGETAL, HERBAL, CITRUS, TROPICAL, DRIED FRUIT, BITTER, SPICY, SWEET, CHOCOLATE, CARAMEL, COFFEE, NUTTY, SMOKY

ADDITIONAL NOTES

FINAL RATING

- APPEARANCE ☆☆☆☆☆
- TASTE ☆☆☆☆☆
- MOUTHFEEL ☆☆☆☆☆
- OVERALL RATING ☆☆☆☆☆

🥃 NAME			
🏭 DISTILLERY		🍾 TYPE	
🌐 ORIGIN		🛢 AGE	
💲 PRICE		📅 SAMPLED	

COLOR METER

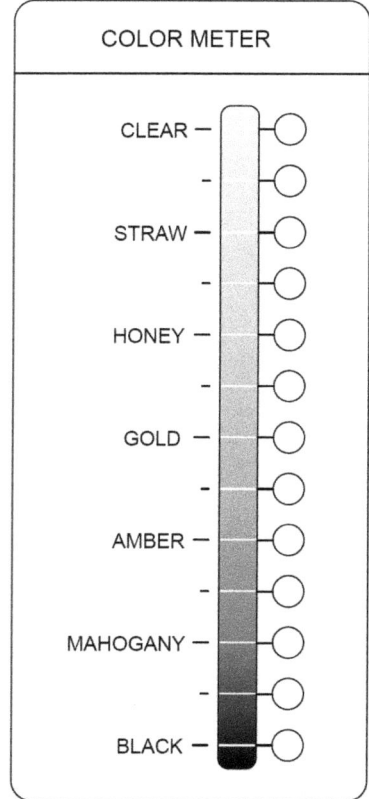

- CLEAR
- STRAW
- HONEY
- GOLD
- AMBER
- MAHOGANY
- BLACK

FLAVOR WHEEL

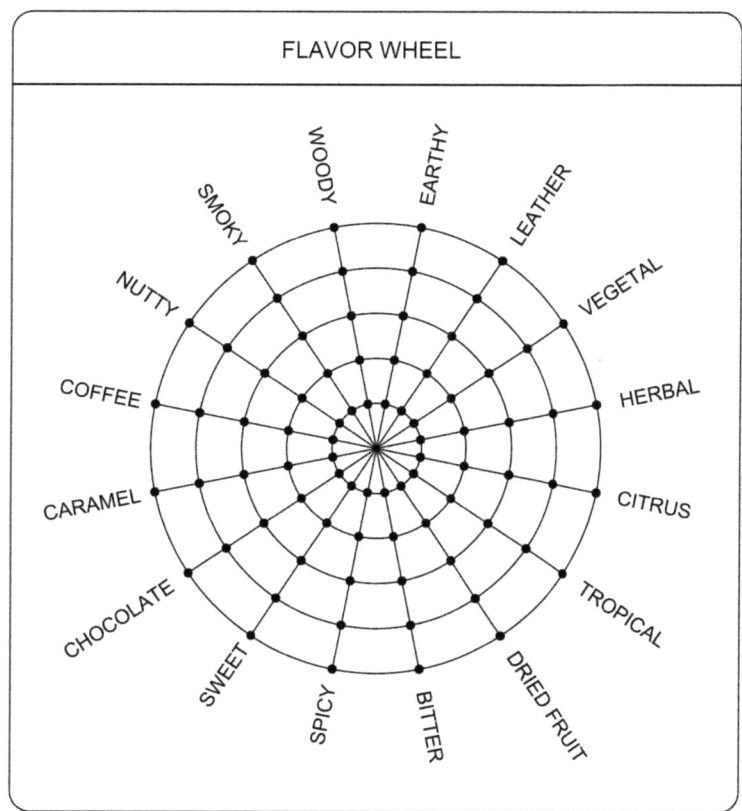

WOODY, EARTHY, LEATHER, VEGETAL, HERBAL, CITRUS, TROPICAL, DRIED FRUIT, BITTER, SPICY, SWEET, CHOCOLATE, CARAMEL, COFFEE, NUTTY, SMOKY

ADDITIONAL NOTES

FINAL RATING

- 🍾 APPEARANCE ☆☆☆☆☆
- 👅 TASTE ☆☆☆☆☆
- 👄 MOUTHFEEL ☆☆☆☆☆
- ⭐ OVERALL RATING ☆☆☆☆☆

NAME			
DISTILLERY		TYPE	
ORIGIN		AGE	
PRICE		SAMPLED	

COLOR METER

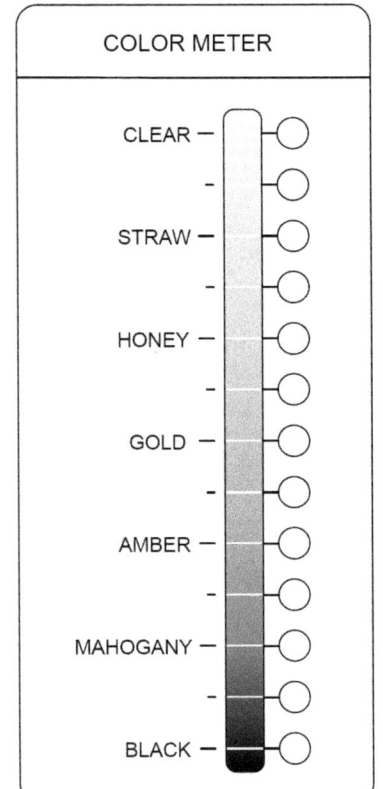

- CLEAR
- STRAW
- HONEY
- GOLD
- AMBER
- MAHOGANY
- BLACK

FLAVOR WHEEL

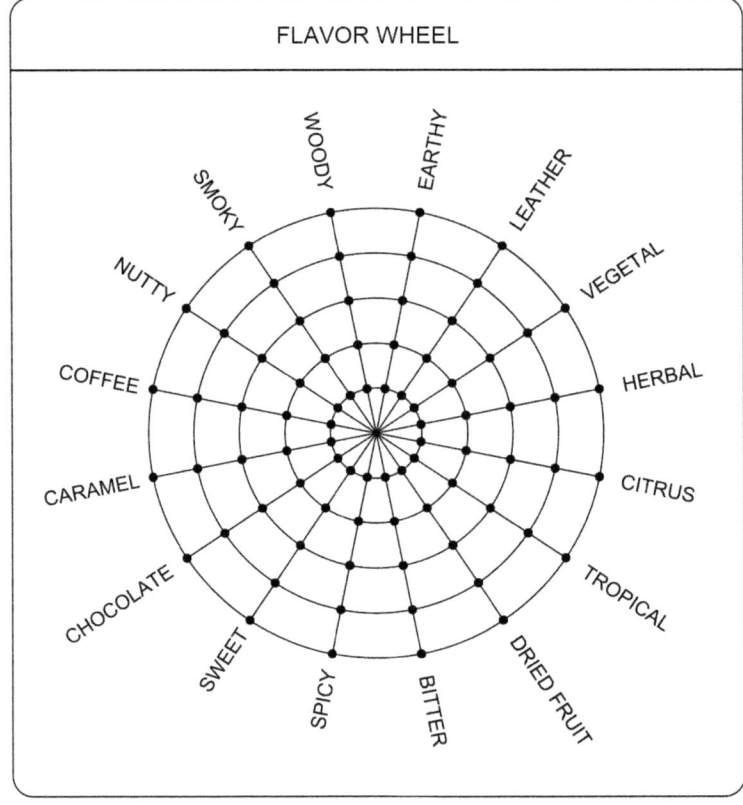

SMOKY, WOODY, EARTHY, LEATHER, VEGETAL, HERBAL, CITRUS, TROPICAL, DRIED FRUIT, BITTER, SPICY, SWEET, CHOCOLATE, CARAMEL, COFFEE, NUTTY

ADDITIONAL NOTES

FINAL RATING

- APPEARANCE ☆☆☆☆☆
- TASTE ☆☆☆☆☆
- MOUTHFEEL ☆☆☆☆☆
- OVERALL RATING ☆☆☆☆☆

Lightning Source UK Ltd.
Milton Keynes UK
UKHW051233210820
368606UK00007B/735